To Stop Extinction

Tom Carr

To Stop Extinction

Contents

To Stop Extinction

Introduction

A couple years ago, I wasn't expecting anything, and I received a very interesting transmission. This is the book The 5000 Year Message. It arrived in a two hour period one evening in September. I took the dictation after I came back to earth from off-world and didn't know what to do with it, so I just saved the file. This was the start of a series of transmissions I pushed through.

So, off-world we don't have memos. Memos are something you can say you didn't get. Off-world, information is there, all you do is look for information on a subject and you get everything, more info than you can handle in the next decade if you study full time.

I call this body of information a SYMBOL. I had to pick a name or a description, so symbol works. Symbol in this context means all the information about a subject.

An easy way to think of a symbol is like a neural network where there are a large number of neurons and connections between the neurons can change in strength and number. This universal structure existed before the physical brain and is the model for the brain.

For example, five billion years ago there was no earth or brains upon it, but this symbol structure was already nearly ten billion years in use. On earth we understand a bit about brains, so it's an easy comparison to say that knowledge in the universe is structured like the human brain.

As a dualist, I simply come back from off-world, sit down at the computer, and write down what I remember. I haven't gotten any new transmissions in a while, so maybe this is it and that's fine. I still haven't provided most of the detail, but I've gotten enough for now, and I have the rest of the information if anyone wants it.

Off-world, I guess I would compare myself to a janitor on earth. Hey, I guess someone must do it and I drew the short straw in the forever drawing. The truth I ignore is I'm just a slow learner on a universal scale.

To Stop Extinction

When I was a kid, my family used to go to Huntington Beach in California on summer days. The sun was out, the sand was warm, the water was nice and the waves were big. Everyone liked and loved each other. Those were the best of days.

Because I didn't want them to end, I would stay in the water for one more wave. When everyone was getting ready to leave, I wanted one more wave.

On one trip, everyone had packed up and was in the car and my dad was driving the old Dodge station wagon out of the parking lot and I had to climb into the back as it was moving. I just wanted one more wave, no matter what.

Have you ever wanted something that much? Have you ever had such passion that it overwhelmed you? What can elicit that passion within you? What do you care about so much that you will take action to get it?

On the other hand, I've been here since the last upgrade was done, like forty thousand years ago. Usually, I'm sitting at the back of the room while someone tells us how important they are. They are the going to get whacked, but not before they step all over everyone around them. In all that time, it never has ended well for that person, but the next guy does the same thing. It appears to be an error in the human design, that ego gets inflated proportionate to power, but I assume there is a reason for this design specification.

When I announce off-world I would like to transmit some symbols down to earth, the entities barely look up, the cadres ignore me: "You know the designer's crew has a plan and they are taking care of this, right?"

Yeah, yeah, I know. John Cusack once lamented something like, "no one likes my puppet show." Well, it was a role he delivered, but I identified with him. We could have been contenders.

I'm not being "given" this information. Because I'm active off-world, I can access it just like anyone else off-world, the Archives are always there, the Symbols are always there. Because I'm a dualist, I can stuff it in my mind and retrieve it a bit better than other people, only losing maybe half of it. The secret I know is that if enough of you understand the truth, we can create a portal and get really good things. Lots and lots of really good things you would truly love.

I'm not the only one working on this, though maybe I'm the only one to put it in your face. So, you may hear about some of the stuff I talk about from one place or another. Don't worry about it, the stuff is in the ether, there are lots of us working on the same project. If someone says the same things I'm saying, they are accessing the same Symbol. Their ego may tell them to claim they figured out the universe. I've been there, too, and so will you. Nod and smile, all good.

I've been waiting decades for transmissions, but no one sent me anything. So, I just started doing it myself when I go off-world and come back. My associates off-world say I wasn't ready, or it wasn't the right time before. Whatever.

I've used the symbols I can access to write three books detailing a projection which is a composite of several probable realities. So, I have access to probable realities off-world. It's easy to get access to whichever probable reality matches your vibration or perspective. So, when someone has a near death experience, they are tethered to their body on earth with a silver cord. My dear hero, Yogananda, was able to sever his silver cord from off-world and die just to show the western world how it works. So, these people are dead for a minute and get access to the probable reality which most closely aligns with their vibration. They see what is best for them to see, most often they see the beauty off-world, a religious experience, or a future which is a probable reality. Probable reality does not mean it is the most probable reality, it means given values for specific variables, this is the most likely future.

In my off-world review of probable realities, I have access to more than one probable reality. The one that I resonated with most was the one where we get a wonderful world, even though seven out of ten I looked at were extinction one way or another.

So, as a liaison, I'm presenting what I see as the transmission of symbols which are the antidote to several probable realities which end in human extinction. It was surprising to me. I did not expect that human extinction was impending. You hear about it off-world, but unless the probable reality is the one you hope for, you blow off the rest. This book is To Stop Extinction. I had no plans for such a book or title until it arrived over the course of a couple months.

It's not likely, simply because a good number of humans have to want to be wealthy and secure instead of suffering, and they don't know they have a choice. It will take at least 1 out of every 200 American adults. I hope I can show you how you make a choice instead of being a victim. This is not a creating wealth pep talk; this is a nice tool which is activation of mass consciousness. I'm not sure I'm good enough at this stuff to do it, but I'm going to try. I figure at least you should know this option exists and it's simple to make happen. I brought this option back from off-world because I'm tired of the way some people run this planet, it's not fair and results in extinction.

The 5000 Year Message is the first document of the projection. I was given the assembled version of a guide to being human delivered over the last 5000 years. This delivery was in four events by the designer of humans. My naming of the designer of humans is a functional personification. You can choose any name which you feel is appropriate for the power or consciousness or part of the universe which designed humans.

These four events were for the purpose of delivering a message. These messages were delivered through the best human available at the time for the specific message. Each of the four events resulted in a major religion. These religions are Hinduism, Buddhism, Taoist, and Christianity. In The 5000 Year Message, we assemble these four parts into one, which becomes more than the parts: a guide for being human and understanding your experience of life on earth. The assembled message is only about 25 words.

I don't know why the message hadn't been assembled before, these pieces have been lying around for the longest time. Maybe it has been assembled before. It's just common knowledge off-world. As well, I have no idea why I got the transmission, it's not like I'm in the loop on anything big off-world. Still, I think it's cool I did get it, and I hope I have delivered it properly.

In the second book, A Definition of Human Rights, we define human rights from an off-world perspective: there are 25 human rights. Your task is to choose which of these 25 human rights you want for yourself and your family. Your only assurance of getting these rights is if everyone gets these rights. A method of advantage is only temporary because it only benefits you, and we call this mindset Advantagist.

In this third book, To Stop Extinction, we provide examples of Simple Systems which are based on the definitions of human rights. These systems bring wealth and security to everyone. Properly executed, the need for advantage is superseded by wealth and security for everyone. We provide a plan for implementation which provides a good chance of stopping extinction.

The first part of this book is Simple Systems. So, as we all know, we humans do things ass-backwards. The good news is that it is pretty simple to fix if you want to be wealthy and secure. By you, I mean a group of humans. Yeah, I know, don't hold your breath. Humans would have to participate. Ouch, deal breaker.

The third part is a plan to stop extinction, you know, something like a 12- step. How do we get out of this mess. Potentially. Not likely, not even being considered, barely possible. But that's all I have for you. Sorry in advance. The odds are against us.

In all three books, the fourth part, Foundation, is the same. The Foundation is basic off-world information. This is so that anyone can get one book but can get the same overview of the off-world program. While I know this does not follow traditional book publishing concepts, my presentation is not compromised by those traditions, though I do love books.

These off-world books are not static, completed documents, but instead are versioned documents with progressive editions if changes are made. The versioning of the foundation will be noted by number and date, such as Edition 1 July 2022 and then Edition 2 December 2023, etc.

After the basic information in the Foundation, there is a bit about me, so you don't ask who the Hell wrote this. It's at the very end of the book. If you get that far, you may glance over it and close the cover. Fair enough. This section includes my simple description of duality, a bit about my self-appointed role as liaison, and a description of symbols and how I transmit symbols from off-world to earth.

We humans are hurling undauntedly towards extinction and destruction of earth, generally without concern.

The off-world perspective is that 2/3 of species such as humans destroy their planet and themselves. So pending destruction is not a surprise but rather a likelihood. And it is the 11th hour for humans.

At the same time, 1/3 of species like humans don't destroy themselves. The off-world community is reaching out to help us understand how.

To Stop Extinction

At this point, we face the final test for a free will species. This test is to overcome your instinct to survive without concern for others and instead participate as a part of a whole, the human beings of earth. By design, the tribal instinct is normally weaker than your instinct to survive. The perspective to which we transition is that for any of us to survive, we must all get the same opportunity. If you only focus on your own survival, eventually as a species you destroy the planet because everyone feels their survival is a valid reason to grab whatever they need or want. That time is happening now.

Humans must make this transition in their minds. If we don't, the odds are we will go extinct. So, this is a test of the species design. Are our minds good enough to see the value of others instead of ignoring others? It is within our power to do this, but will we? The answer so far is no.

The purpose of this projection by the off-world community is to offer the means to improve the lives of humans and fix the planet.

In the movie The Day the Earth Stood Still, the arrival of an alien causes global trauma and chaos. We want to fix things but avoid the global trauma and chaos and general killing-off of humans. Any human can scoff at this offer. Scoffing may not be nice, but it doesn't cause global trauma and chaos.

It may make a good movie that heaven opens, and an angel shows us the way, or a spaceship arrives in Central Park, but there's gonna be some chaos. How can it be done without chaos and getting the kids all traumatized? Get a local to make their offer. I guess that would be me.

The off-world community is offering you wealth, a better quality of life, incredible technology, amazing, large scale environmental solutions, and solutions to social problems.

Right now, I have access to about 50 technologies. I don't have them sitting at home, I have access, I can get them in the right situation. Now, some may show up in the meantime, as I said, I'm not the only circus in town. They are giving this stuff away. So, that's a pretty good deal. I'm just the liaison, a facilitator or broker.

It will take some work to save this species and fixing the planet will take a lot of work. To explain what is offered and available, I have a bunch of transmissions which is basically notes about symbols. Each transmission could be a book, they say. To expedite the delivery, I am providing a short version of the concepts in this third book, To Stop Extinction.

You may wonder: if the off-world community can put an end to human suffering, why wouldn't they just do so? That is why you are reading this. First, that was tried before and didn't work. It's before the history in our books, but I was there. Humans didn't change. This time, I am one of the boats coming for people on their roof during the flood. I'm probably not what you expected nor hoped for, but here I am, nonetheless.

So, here is a quick fix which we will go into detail about in the Foundation. With these 7 words, 3 steps you take with your mind, you save the world:

Be sincere.

Be honest.

Support Human Rights.

For example, if everyone used these 7 words as their guide, what problem is not corrected? It's not that difficult of a concept. The challenge is in personal conversion and application, i.e., believing it and doing it. As with all activations, we must implement a process with a large enough group of people to achieve manifestation. This is detailed in Part 2 of this book.

To Stop Extinction

Humans must show that they want to continue as a species. Why would the off-world community save humans if humans aren't interested in saving themselves? Please, give yourself a better future, take a small leap even if you're not sure, allow us to show you that off-world we are sincere and honest.

Each of you are invited to participate in projects about which you feel strongly. Your passion can be stronger than anything on this earth. Let us show you how.

I could have a fancy hard-wired communication bridge to off-world: a portal. That would be great. I know how it's done. But I'm on a tight budget, so I have a sort of ET phone home set up, it works now and then, intermittent with a bunch of distortion. And off-world distortion isn't just fuzzy reception, we're not talking about puny radio waves anymore.

With my comm bridge I can provide proof on your terms. I can get you 30 minutes of un-diluted truth which can change everything for you. Proof on your terms. You decide: what would it take to prove it to you? You can ask the off-world operatives when I get you connected, and this provides the proof on your terms.

To Stop Extinction

It would be nice if someone wanted to open a portal to the galaxy. I have listed all the tech we can get, probably worth trillions in this economy.

So, if anyone reads this, there you have it. I brought the best, coolest symbols and probable realities to earth.

Thank you for giving us your time and consideration even if you decide against stopping extinction.

If you decide to save humans, sign up and participate, make a ten minute investment in the fate of humanity.

Tom

Christmas Eve, 2022

Part 1- Simple Systems

Simplicity enables transparency which enables honesty. This is the concept of Simple Systems. Dishonesty is camouflaged with complexity. A Simple System may not include all manner of exception, but the most important understanding is that with Simple Systems everyone knows how things work and everyone can have an important voice in how things work.

If you are part of complexity, a reset is to focus upon clear, transparent, honest, and simple methods, interactions, and communications. These are true goals of any interaction or civilization. If you do not understand this now, you will in the future. These concepts are the basis of Simple Systems.

Simple is the highest priority, other priorities cannot sacrifice simplicity. The concepts presented here are simple, but there may be even simpler systems which will have greater success, so these Simple Systems are just examples so that people can understand that simplicity is possible and can enable wealth and security for all.

We use the term Advantagist to mean an individual who seeks advantage over others. The Advantagist model is that when survival becomes likely due to the development of civilization, the instinct to survive is not diminished and converted to a focus on tribal instincts. Instead, this instinct was converted to obtaining advantage over others.

It is still approved of and suggested that one do what one can to get ahead. This concept creates the "rat race". To paraphrase As Jack Reacher, do these people look like they are free?

Basically, if you are getting ahead, it is not in a vacuum, you are getting an advantage over others, which means they are dis-advantaged. By getting ahead, you are leaving others behind. This is why many Americans feel left behind. The Advantagists are aware of this, their intention may not have been to leave others behind, or maybe it was. But their intention was to gain advantage over others. If someone characterizes this differently, they are being dishonest.

Once the civilization achieved general survival, instead of diminishing the instinct to survive, it was transitioned into Advantagist methods which led to cartels. In an Advantagist environment, cartels are groups of people who seek disproportionate financial advantage. These cartels are based on profession or industry. These people do not refer to themselves as cartels. They might characterize themselves as professionals who worked hard to get ahead.

The instinct to survive was not diminished because of economic accretion mechanisms. Later, A Stable Economy presents the concept of a developed economy as an accretion model. Accretion is a word in our presentation for financial concentration. The accretion takes place by many groups, all working on an Advantagist model. So, we would suggest that each cartel is an accretion method.

The way we look at this off-world is to look at result. Then the mechanisms used to achieve the result can be determined. So, in the American culture, you have more than 50% of the wealth owned by 1% of the population. So, if there are 250 million adults, then 2.5 million adults have more than 50% of the wealth.

We are not concerned with that wealth which already exists. We seek to assist you in creating wealth for you and everyone else.

Re-distribution of wealth is not part of this project. Re-distribution of wealth is based on a scarcity which is inaccurate. We would not suggest taking anything from anyone.

But, for example, if we give wealth to everyone, we have not taken from the wealthy. Giving poor people wealth in the form of welfare or handouts is not our model. We mention this here because many people are very frightened that a government may take what they own. This type of confiscation takes place constantly around the world, so this is not without rationale. Confiscation is not part of our model.

In America, a common method is to suggest some idea is socialism or communism to cause distrust. Off-world, there is no socialism, communism, or capitalism. These are outdated concepts of social and economic models from prior centuries, so this exposes a position removed from the reality.

This is a dishonesty almost always based on fear. At some point, the individual became frightened of their survival or wealth being taken, and this is the basis of such assertions. Their fear is not completely without reason. The purpose of this off-world presentation is to provide security or to

4

increase security, not to diminish security. This includes financial security.

There is only support of human rights and to what extent human rights are supported. A country may present that they tax people heavily to provide a basic standard of living to all citizens. This model, however, does not deal with underlying accretion methods.

We use the word accretion to mean financial concentration, meaning the concentration of financial assets, the concentration of wealth.

A financial instrument might simply be a check from a bank, but in this case we use the term instrument for a system for financial concentration.

There are two accretion instruments which are common to all in America. These are real estate and stock markets.

In addition, industry specific cartels have developed to enable Advantagist behavior. The formation of a cartel enables the members the achieve an economic advantage over everyone else. In America, these cartels are usually based on profession or industry.

While these instruments are technically available to all citizens, the result of these instruments is that 1% of the population acquire more than 50% of the wealth.

A simple example is that while you can buy real estate and sell it for profit, the bulk of mortgage payments are for interest. So, while you may enter a higher asset level through real estate, you typically cannot get around the bulk of your mortgage payment is profit to others.

The cartels as accretion instruments work simply by enabling the participant to earn more than other people earn. So, four years of education enables doubling your lifetime income. As lifetime income is commonly thought of as forty years, the concept is that forgoing income for 10% of those years doubles the total overall yield. For cartels, additional education can yield another doubling or more. This concept is unsustainable and is unnecessary. If you remember history, Abraham Lincoln was a poor country lawyer. Some time back, doctors made house calls. These Advantagist cartels did not start creating the current situation until the 1960's.

16 Simple Systems

The purpose of the Simple Series is to provide a simple solution to an issue. The implementation of these systems can provide equality. No one will be left behind, and no one will be part of an underclass of poverty. This does not mean we have to take anything from anyone. There is a basic dishonest assertion by the Advantagists, who are commonly called Elites by some, and that assertion is that everyone can successfully become an Advantagist. This does not respect and appreciate people as they are nor the nature of our country. This model is dishonest.

If you have benefited from such advantage, you should be intelligent to recognize that you have incredible economic advantage over most people and that a country cannot succeed with such dishonesty. In simple terms, we don't want to take from you, we want to provide a way to succeed for those who don't have your abilities. This will benefit you as well, because your wealth becomes more secure when no one needs your wealth. If everyone is secure, there is much less risk that your wealth will be taken something from you.

In this document, we have detailed 16 simple issues which can change the world.

A human culture has a method for handling these simple issues which developed over time, typically without overt human conceptualization. As well, humans have their own ideas about any given issue.

Here are the Simple Systems provided in this document:

1.   Simple Land

2.   Simple Communities (Neighborhoods, Villages, Cities)

3.   Simple Home

4.   Simple Pay

5.   Simple Tax

6.   Simple Government

7.   Simple Farming

8.   Simple Immigration

9.   Simple Vote

10. Simple Employment

11. Simple Working Relationship

12. Simple Retirement

13. Simple Natural Resources

14. Simple Law

There are lots of other simple concerns and we have access to those symbols, so the list can grow or change. In this document, we will provide models for the most important of Simple Systems based on human rights. All the human rights which are not interpreted in a Simple System can be dealt with later. The conversion to Simple Systems we present in this document would change our culture and enable the next steps in a plan to stop extinction, but we are not there yet.

So, there are many more Simple Systems. If a system is not in this list, it doesn't mean it isn't important, but these Simple Systems will change everyone's life. Specifically, groups which focus upon themselves might feel we did not address their specific issues. These first Simple Systems are universal and will change everything for everyone. If these changes are done, all the rest of the unfair systems can be corrected, too.

Benefits of Simple Systems

Here are the benefits to you from adopting the Simple Systems:

1.   Simple Land. You get land to live upon for your lifetime without cost.

2.   Simple Communities.

a.   Neighborhoods and villages. By making neighborhoods and villages small and separate, we provide a greater level of security.

b.   Simple City.   A simple city enables democracy, where you have a say in the government, not government where you have no say.

3.   Simple Home. You could get 100 year financing at 0% for a basic home. This could be a mortgage as low as $83 a month compared to thousands a month which is now common.

4.   Simple Pay. Your pay rate is at least 1/7 of the maximum pay anyone in the organization gets but could be ½ of the maximum pay anyone gets.

5.   Simple Tax. Tax is taken as a percentage of sales from business, so there is no income tax for people or business, no property tax, no sales tax or no gas tax, no other taxes. The confusion of taxes is how politicians evade transparency.

6.   Simple Government. Currently, we have taxation without representation, which is not sustainable. As well, the representatives are so removed from citizens they don't have to pay attention to what is important to citizens. These issues are easily corrected with simple government.

7.   Simple Farming. Farming is recognized as the means to survival, so farming and food processing are the one industry which is given special status, with this we can all continue to survive.

8.   Simple Immigration. This enables citizens to benefit from immigration, not just companies. This enables people who want to come to this country to get work visas, a permit to be here if they have a job which benefits the citizens.

9.   Simple Vote. You vote on spending money, not electing politicians. So, for example, you might

vote to increase defense spending or not. Politicians control money, this is a bad idea.

10.   Simple employment.   With simple employment, everyone can get a job and be productive: old, young, minorities...everyone.

11.   Simple Working Relationship. With simple working relationship you get all the benefits of being a contractor. You work your own schedule so can have the life you want right now, you don't have to wait for retirement to take off a week, a month or a season.

12.   Simple Retirement. With simple retirement, people are not forced to retire. Seniors have the freedom to work or not. If they want to work, they can do so based on their ability, not their age.

13.   Simple Natural Resources.   With simple natural resources, the citizens of the country own the natural resources through re-purchase. If the resources are to be sold or used, the citizens of the country are the ones who benefit, using contractors to do the work such as pumping, mining, drilling and processing.

14.   Simple Law. With Simple Law, laws will be simple, easy to read and understand, and a law might be 25 words in plain English.

Simple Land

Land to live on is included in A Definition of Human Rights.

Earth was given to man. You may not agree, but your agreement is not required. This could also be said as earth is home to humans.

If you are born on earth, if you live, there is no doubt this includes a place to live, and this is normally provided by your parents until you reach adulthood.

As a concept, it is easy to understand that every human being has a birthright to a place to live.

In America, the negation of this is part of the economic accretion or concentration which creates advantage and therefore inequality.

The Off-World economic perspective looks at results and works backwards to determine what happened. In the case of America, about 1% of the population own greater than 50% of the wealth.

To Stop Extinction

This inequity is historically about the point when revolutions occur.

The birthright to a place to live can be understood to be land to live on while you are alive.

Existing ownership of land is not disputed nor changed.

In the American model, land is owned, and that ownership can be passed on to others. This is unethical, individuals cannot own the earth, all humans own the earth. The overthrow of any government or regime eliminates all prior ownership. This has happened for every government or regime in human history, so this is part of a complete description.

That said, a keystone of these projections is that nothing is taken from anyone. This means, in this context, that no ownership of land is taken from anyone. If some land is owned by someone and the culture decides the land should be used differently, the current model of eminent domain is functional. I would add, for security, that market rates should be paid for any land acquired through the application of eminent domain.

We want to implement the human birthright of land with the least trauma to the culture, and so we would assume that all land which is owned in accordance with American law remain so. So, put simply, we are not suggesting that the land you own be taken from you. Just the opposite, we are asserting that the land you own is not taken from you. As people have great fear about this, it is not possible to allay those fears, as fear is not rational nor reasonable. So, even if the next one hundred pages only repeated the statement "The land you own will not be taken from you without market rate payment", it would not allay those fears, as there is no allaying of such fears.

The birthright we are suggesting would be implemented on land which is not currently in use or can be acquired through purchase. There is adequate land which is not in used to implement this program. So, Birthright Land is defined as land which is currently not in use or can be acquired through purchase.

Land which is not used can potentially be considered as eligible for Birthright land. However, there are many considerations in this process.

The allocation of the birthright land would end with your death. This means you will receive the land at the time of adulthood if you wish, and the land would go back to be used by another who is reaching adulthood after you die. In this model, whatever mortgage for the basic housing would be taken on by the next person.

This would establish a pool of available land to which adults can request as their Birthright Land.

As the Birthright Land is land to live upon, residence would be expected. If you wish to reside elsewhere, you will normally give up the Birthright land you are not going to use for residence. If you decide you want Birthright Land to live upon later, you would be able to receive an available piece of land.

There would have to be a process and protocols for this disbursement. For example, when a parent dies, an adult child may give up their Birthright Land if they want to reside on the parent's Birthright Land.

In this model, there would be no property tax for Birthright Land. Refer to Simple Tax for details on a tax model.

A culture could use any size for birthright land. However, that size should apply to all birthright land assignments, so everyone gets the same size plot of birthright land.

In this model, we would suggest 1/8 of an acre. An acre is 43,560 square feet, so this would be 5445 square feet. For simplicity, 5000 square feet might be used as birthright land. This would set an acre as being 8 assignments of birthright land with common and access areas. However, this could be decided by states. States with a lot of land might offer a larger plot.

A couple of humans who live together most often reside in one location. So, the second person would not need Birthright Land. However, people move in and move out, so it would have to be decided when the Birthright Land is relinquished. As well, re-acquisition of Birthright Land would need to be simple and automatic. Perhaps for a couple, two adjacent plots could be allocated to a couple, but this would have to consider availability. These decisions would be up to the culture or state to decide how to administrate.

There are over 200 million adults in America. Many may not want nor need birthright land. However, the maximum amount of land needed should be allocated. 200 million divided by 8 per acre is 25 million acres. As there are 640 acres in a square mile, 25 million acres is about 39,000 square miles. For ease of discussion, we could say 40,000 square miles is needed to give every adult American 1/8 of an acre of birthright land.

America has about 3.8 million square miles. Birthright Land would be about 1% of total land in America. Not all land is usable, such as mountain ranges, so birthright land would be a larger percentage of usable land. But stillthis is not a large percentage of land, this is a relatively inconsequential amount of land. The significance to Americans, on the other hand, is dramatic.

Simple Communities

The organization of Simple Land into neighborhoods, villages and cities takes advantage of human nature to provide levels of security. A more detailed description and drawings are provided here for transparency. These could be a basis but are just an example.

8 Plot Acre

This drawing shows 8 plots on an acre as an example.

Each plot is 50 feet by 100 feet, or 5000 square feet.

There is a common road or driveway which is 12 to 25 feet wide.

There is a common border area on the end of each plot. This could be for utility access, for example.

8 residences with an American average of 2.6 people per household would be about 21 people per acre.

While American residential developments offer more, homes might be sold for $500,000. The citizens of a state can decide what makes sense to them.

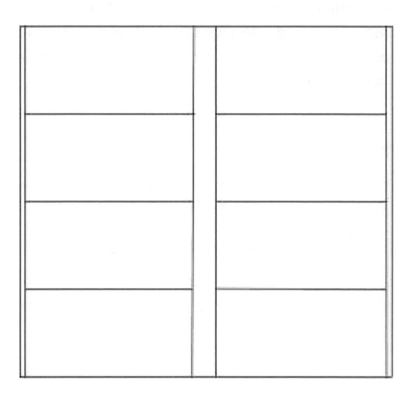

8 Acre Neighborhood

Eight of the 8 Plot Acres can be designed to be a 64 plot, 8-acre neighborhood.

In this example, 4 plots are allocated to be a common area, such as a playground, pool, or clubhouse. This leaves 60 plots. At 2.6 people per household, this is 156 people in a neighborhood. Instinctive tribal design is about 144 people per tribe, so this would take advantage of natural tribal inclination, creating a tribe which is the residents of the neighborhood. Basically, everyone can know everyone who lives is the neighborhood.

A common road is used, which is 24 feet wide and about 878 feet long, so about 21,000 square feet, close to one half acre, so this example of a neighborhood would be 60 plots using about 8.5 acres, about 424 feet by 878 feet.

While modern urban design has a different aesthetic, the concept here is that this is free. The second concept is that with human nature in mind, this creates a neighborhood.

To Stop Extinction

As a neighborhood, there could be a wall around the neighborhood with access from only one side or the other enabling security to control access.

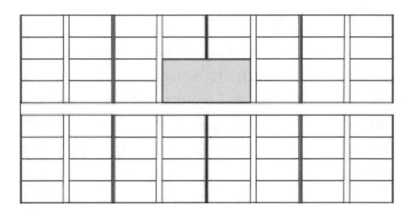

6 Neighborhood Village

6 neighborhoods could be designated a village, and access could be limited to one point for security. So there could be one access point to a village, and one access point to each neighborhood in the village.

This would have 360 residences. With an average of 2.6 people per household, this would be 936 people in the village.

In this example, a common road of 36 feet width connects the neighborhoods.

The area would be 1792 feet by 1272 feet, about 52 acres.

What is important is that about 1000 people have a place to live which can be safe and doesn't cost them anything, and it only takes about 52 acres.

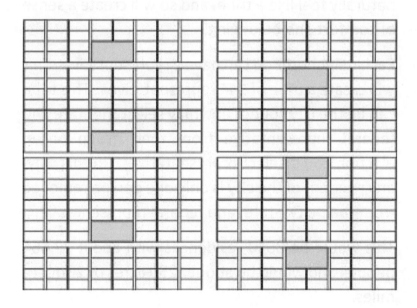

Simple City

24 Village City

24 villages can be a city. This would consist of 6 neighborhoods per village, and so would be a total of 144 neighborhoods. The neighborhood will naturally feel like a tribe, and so will create a sense of comfort and belonging.

Each neighborhood can have a representative. This will create a tribe of 144 representatives. This tribe can be the city council and may select the state and federal representative from their group or an election could select representatives. In this way, any resident of the city is only one person removed from their city, state, and federal representative.

This would be 8640 residences with about 22,464 people, and would be about 1250 acres or 2 square miles.

To Stop Extinction

This does not include schools, commercial and industrial space.

Schools

In this city example of 22,464 people, there would be about 10% in elementary school. This would be about 2200 children. So if there were one elementary school for 370 children, that would be 6 elementary schools. If they are 5 acres each, that is 30 acres.

If there are 3% in middle school, that would be about 700 kids, which might be 2 schools with 10 acres each.

If there are 7% in high school, that would be about 1500 kids, which might be 1 high school with 30 acres.

That would be about 70 acres for schools.

Commercial and Industrial Space

There are about 100 billion square feet of commercial space in the USA, which is about 500 square feet per person, so a city of 20,000 would need about 200 acres for commercial and industrial space. However, this varies, it could be double that amount, so we will simply allocate 400 acres.

Commercial space could be provided by splitting the 24 neighborhoods north-south or east-west and put the commercial space in-between.

Industrial space could be zoned outside the neighborhood boundaries, so it surrounded the city.

Public Property

Parks and public buildings might be 100 acres for a city of 20,000.

Utilities

While utility providers and city buildings and yards can be in industrial areas, space could also be allocated in each neighborhood. This might be one or two plots. This would enable neighborhood utilities which might include a well and tank storage, solar or wind, and an electrical sub-station. Creating self-sufficient neighborhoods reduces infrastructure.

Total City Land

In this example of a city which is based on 144 times 144, a city might be between twenty and twenty-five thousand residents.

The home plots and access roads are about 1250 acres.

Schools are about 70 acres.

Public Property is about 100 acres.

Commercial and Industrial space is about 400 acres.

The total acreage is 1820 acres. 3 square miles is 1920 acres, so allocation of 3 square miles should be a good model.

Rather than enlarging a city beyond this level, it is better to have a different city. The reason has to do with tribal instincts. 150 residents will have a neighborhood that satisfies the instinctive definition of a tribe and can enable comfort between people in their neighborhood. If each neighborhood has a resident as it's representative, then

In this model an urban area would consist of 3 square mile areas, though smaller cities would be fine, too.

To Stop Extinction

The drawing shows center strips going north-south and east-west separating the city into 6 village quarters. These central areas could be used for schools, parks, public buildings, and commercial space. The drawing shows external areas for industrial space. This is an example of a 3 square mile city with perhaps 22,000 residents.

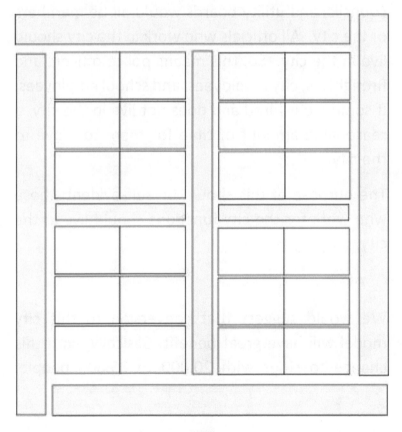

Local Staffing

All public agencies should be staffed by the citizens of the city. So, this means school boards, city councils, and utility boards would all be members of the city. All officials who work in the city should live in the city. So, this means police officers and firefighters, city employees, and school employees. If someone is hired and does not live in the city, a reasonable amount of time for them to move to the city.

The purpose of this should be self-evident: those who work for the city functions should live in the city.

Conversion

We would suggest that conversion to this city model will have great benefit. Basically, with this change to cities with 20,000 to 25,000 people, citizens go from having no power to having all the power. This should be enough incentive.

To convert a city to this model:

1.	The city should be separated into areas of the appropriate population. This should be done in a simple way. If there is 50,000 people in a city, you could separate the city into 2 cities or separate it into 3 cities.

2.	Large cities can still have a city name affiliation, so this could be directional which would yield up to four cities (north, south, east, west). If there are more than 100,000 people in the city, neighborhood names can be used for the cities but still retain the city affiliation, such as West Los Angeles, a neighborhood city of Los Angeles. The separated cities can organize together as suits their needs, such as promotion and events.

3.	Neighborhoods should be identified and named. The neighborhood would benefit from restricting access to a single location. Basically, all that is required for this is stopping through traffic. For this reason, a large or busy street would normally be a separation between smaller cities.

4.	Police and Fire Departments should be within the city.

5.   Schools should be within the city, and the city should have its own school district.

6.   Utilities typically have their own jurisdiction and facilities locations. This should be corrected whenever possible to be located within a city. There should be only one provider of any utility within a city. This relates to natural resources, so Simple Resources specifically addresses this issue.

Simple Home

With Simple Land, you are provided a plot of land to live upon for your life. This would take place when you reach adulthood.

Upon that land you would need a home.

By removing the land purchase from the cost, the cost of the house remains.

One of the many dishonesties in American culture is the depreciation of real estate which is not the long-term truth.

In this concept, we suggest that you think of a home as what we give to ourselves. We each get a home, which is a house, so it is a right to get a home, but the home still has a cost. The earth exists, so, technically we didn't have to pay the universe for the planet. Houses which become our home must be built.

The change in concept is that we, as a culture or country, are helping ourselves to get this home. In this model, we suggest that loans for basic homes be given at no interest.

To obtain the funding for these homes, you could just print money, which is how many countries handle financing, but a better model might be to offer bonds to acquire financing. The interest for these bonds may change. For example, honest bonds for home financing on the world market may need to offer 1% return, or 2% or 3%, perhaps higher. This cost can be covered at the state or federal level. In other words, this rate may vary, so a government may have to supplement the cost to attract investors.

We suggest no interest loans for basic houses with the interest of bonds paid by the government through Simple Tax. These loans could also be offered at 1-3%. This rate could be set by the citizens. But I would suggest, after defense and governmental expenses, Simple Home mortgages are the most important expense of a government. T government expenses would include funding of executive, legislative and judicial expenses. We will present this in another Simple section, Simple Tax.

Home funding is the most important expense after defense and government expense because this is how we get a place to live. If we have a place to live, we have security and can be at peace. At least it's possible.

House funding is normally done at 30 or sometimes 15 years. This is inaccurate. A home will last more than 100 years. Even if the house is not properly maintained, restoring a home is usually more reasonable than building a new one. So, in this model, home funding should be for 100 years at 0%.

Home construction is usually done on-site. This should change as well. Home construction can be done at a factory and the home moved to a site. This is how manufactured homes, mobile homes, and tiny homes are built. This is more economical, and standards can be set to insure adequate quality. For those who work in home construction, I would suggest this means you work at a local home factory in your city and no longer commute to a jobsite.

I would suggest that a basic home be eligible for this funding. If a larger home or additions are needed, that is handled separately and not part of the basic Simple Home model. So, this home might be 1000 square feet or 1200 square feet, or more. This is up to the citizens of a country or state to decide. For example, a 1000 square foot 2-

bedroom, 2 bathroom home with a living room, kitchen, dining room. A 3rd bedroom or a family room might be included if a larger size is allowed, and a garage can be included.

The cost for this example might be $100,000, and so we will use an example of $100,000 loans for 100 years at 0% interest. This would mean a principal payment of $1000 a year, which is $83 a month.

For a 1% interest rate on $100,000 over 100 years, the payment is $131. For 2% interest, the payment is $192. Traditional loans of $100,000 for 30 years with 3% interest would be $421 a month. So, the residents of a country or state can decide for themselves how to finance. If you start with traditional loans with a 3% rate, you could progressively lower that rate as the program developed. For some, a 15 year loan might be preferred, for $100,000 at 3%, the payment would be $690.

Because you may not live in the home for 100 years, the property would be available as free land when you die. If your spouse or a relative of yours wants to execute their land right for this property, they would inherit the loan payment at well. When the loan is paid, the property would simply come with a home and there would be no cost. Until the mortgage is paid, whoever is the next occupant of the lands pays the basic home mortgage. Any additional construction on the property would not be part of the basic home mortgage.

Simple Pay

There are several accretion instruments which are ways that wealth is concentrated for a small percentage. Inequity in pay has always been one of them.

Correcting this is relatively easy, and we can assist in this. However, humans are unable to do this simple task, or they would have done it. If there is interest in achieving this, then people will want it. Currently, people don't want this, however, if you change your mind, this can be achieved. If enough people sign up for Simple Pay, we can get this started.

We do not suggest laws to set a maximum pay, minimum pay or to equalize pay. These will not succeed. There is a minimum wage, but this is not adequate, for example.

We don't recommend labor unions. While a century ago labor unions were useful to stop genocidal company, unions are just a poor return high-priced intermediary now.

We suggest a 7:1 pay ratio as a starting point, which means that the lowest paid person in an organization receives 1/7th the pay of the highest paid person in the organization. For example, if the highest paid person in an organization gets $70 an hour, the lowest paid would get $10 an hour. The reason this is suggested is that currently, a 100,000:1 ratio is not that rare, so 7:1 is a very big change.

We calculate it this way because that is how the calculation will be done by an organization. The highest paid person will figure out how much they must pay the lowest, and the adjustments will begin.

A smaller pay ratio is even better, so in a 5:1 pay ratio organization where the highest paid person gets $70 an hour, the lowest paid gets $14 an hour.

With a 3:1 pay ratio organization where the highest paid person gets $70 an hour, the lowest paid person would get $23. You could eventually use 2:1 ratio or 1.5:1 ratio.

We suggest that every employee of an organization gets the same stock options. This means that a new CEO arriving gets the same stock options everyone else gets. The point is that there is no advantage given here.

This model refers to open and operating companies. At the time of formation, all kinds of deals are made to get talent and financing to get a business going. But all those deals should be done before the time of starting operations or going public with a stock offering.

Simple Government

This model for city organization has implications for city, state, and federal government.

If you live in a rural area, then a county model can be substituted for a city model. This would handle counties with less than 25,000 population as it is. If the population of a county is more than 25,000, then the size is doubled or tripled, etc. So, a county with a population of 70,000 is treated like 3 cities and can be divided as makes sense into 3 areas.

The importance and value of simple models cannot be understated. Complexity is the way things dishonesty is camouflaged. So, properly organized, these issues are simple.

I've seen everyone make dishonest statements on earth, and I'm part of everyone, then admit their dishonesty off-world, but it's too late. Simplicity enables transparency which enables honesty.

In our off-world analysis, we see many who consider themselves to be sincere and honest but are not. Correction of this happens when they confront themselves with their own truth. If someone else tries to confront us, often we just deny the truth. So, this is a process which people do not know exists but is part of off-world work continuously.

Currently, there is great division in the country. This is due to dishonesty and lack of sincerity from those who manipulate ideas for their own benefit. So, the starting point is sincerity and honesty.

Basically, these supposed sides are concerned with different issues. These issues are not really discussed.

So, the first step is the ending of conflict. As conservative voices use conflict as their only issue, this is easily superseded, but the independent and liberal sides do not take advantage of this.

City and County Government

While individual plots of land can be provided, there is significant benefit to lifestyle, commerce, and industry if a city is master planned.

While financial and artistic aesthetics have driven urban planning, a different model works on community based on human nature.

In this model city of about 22,000, we set the city size to be about 144 times 144. The instinctive tribal size for humans is about 144. Basically, this is about how many people you can know in a tribe. If there are more than that, it is hard to know everyone.

To enable representation, each neighborhood could have a person designated to represent them. This could be a formal or informal role. In our example city, there would be 144 neighborhood representatives. The responsibility might be to attend a city meeting and represent your neighborhood once a month. With our current schedules of working ourselves to death, this would be a burden. If we only work a day or two a week, it would be easier to focus on the importance of keeping politicians from administrating poverty.

This is city government. That's it. The city council is large with 144. But every person knows someone from a few houses over who is on the city council. To vote who does this may be a simple neighborhood meeting, each candidate makes their pitch, and a vote is taken.

State Government

As there are 144 neighborhoods in a city, this would be 144 representatives. From these 144 representatives, one person would represent the city to the state government. In this model, any citizen is then only one person away from the state representative. So, there would be about 50 representatives per million people. If a state has 5 million people, this would be 250 in the state legislature.

Federal Government

A second person from the 144 representatives could be the federal representative. So, of the 144 neighborhood representatives in a city, one can be the state representative and one can be the federal representative. In either case, you as a citizen are only removed from these representatives by 1 person, and that person lives in your neighborhood and you may be on a first name basis with them.

So, there would be 10,000 or so of these representatives in the USA. Any citizen would only be a person away from direct contact.

While 10,000 representatives could be seen as unwieldy, the value of having direct contact to government is valuable enough to warrant re-organization. It is a simple system.

For example, the first congress had 65 representatives for a population of 5 million, which is about 1 per 77,000. Today we have 435 for 209 million, which is one per 480,000. By the first congress standards, we should probably have 3000 representatives, not 435. By pushing this to 10,000, every American has direct contact with representation.

While you cannot know 20,000 people, you can have be aware of 144. This would mean any American could contact their neighborhood representative, someone who lives within a block of them, and that representative has direct communications with the city's representative- the person making laws and voting on laws- someone who lives in one of the 24 neighborhoods in their city. The simplicity is the goal, complexity makes improvement difficult.

Transition

Government structure is not perfect, it is an idea or concept. The founding fathers, maybe 100 men, got together 250 years ago and perhaps a dozen or two were focused upon a government design. They did a great job, as everyone knows. At the same time, their concept was based on 13 unequal colonies having a working model. Their mandate was to achieve something all the states would accept along with the writers' concepts. But that doesn't mean the structure was perfect nor permanent.

The current structure of government used in America is not acceptable for the nature of the country. Several prominent voices have concepts about how this can be corrected, and their ideas may be workable.

For relations to other countries, this does not mean isolation., it means different levels of interaction and assistance in human rights. We start any discussion with the issue of supporting human rights. Not being honest until now just means you start now. There may be no way to defend a past. A new mindset is embraced.

You can have relations and interactions and commerce, but until a state or country has human rights, they have not earned the right to exist from their citizens. These governments are a dictatorship, autocracy, or oligarchy structure. These governments will change or fail, it is just a matter of time.

The funding model of the USA is dishonest and so corrections must be implemented before the inequity goes beyond repair. The following suggestions are simple observations. If people are honest, they would deal with these obvious issues. If they do not deal with these issues, they are not honest. It's that simple, don't make honesty more complex than it is. There is typically more concern for personal power or a specific agenda than structural integrity. Supporting human rights is structural integrity.

State's Issues

Basically, the federal government must stop taking responsibility for state issues. This is because the states are not united in their goals. So, the USA can serve as a modern concept of how a large area of the planet can organize.

The process for this is not the federal government taking care of all of the states, it is the federal government not taking care of the states. Let the states take care of themselves, and then their true situation will be understood. Standards can be set at a federal level, and then it is up to the states to make it happen. These standards should be generic, such as only credentialed teachers can teach at schools.

Because of federal organization, the low population states have not had to pay for their state but have had the ability to control the money of larger population states. This is taxation without representation.

Senate

The USA currently has taxation without representation due to the organization of the Senate. Therefore, the Senate provides an opportunity for a specific example of inequality and correction.

The Senate should be re-allocated to a proportional system like the House of Representatives. Every state would have at least 1 senator. This could simply be based on one senator per million residents. If a state has 2 million residents, it gets two senators. If a state has 40 million people, it gets 40 senators. That would be about 280 senators by the latest census.

One senator per quarter million might be about 1000 senators. These concepts of large numbers of government representatives reduce the power of any representative, but also diminish the accountability of representatives.

It may seem that keeping track of 5000 representatives and senators is impossible. But the error is that these people have power when there are ways to manage a country without concentrating power with representatives and senators.

This Senate re-allocation is in the interest of the states with large populations, so the simple correction is that no state funding from the federal government is allocated or put into law until this takes place, which makes the same thing happen.

You can fund the government, defense, and Homeland Security and other mandatory departments. As the rest is not handled equitably, it need not be handled.

So, we have identified the change needed and a way to make it happen. This is just an idea of how this problem can be corrected. Any solution which achieves the purpose is fine.

While small population states will resist because they would lose their voice, their voice is unequal at this time. I would suggest that states take care of their issues. The federal government should stay out of state's management issues and diminish revenue collection accordingly. Let the state's collect and spend that money as they see fit.

Human Rights and Funding

The exception has to do with human rights, which has been a central issue. In other words, human rights is not a state's issue, such as whether to build a bridge, human rights are a human issue. If a state does not recognize human rights, you have a make or break issue.

If teachers must have teaching credentials, this is part of a manifestation of the right to education. A right to education requires that the ability of the teacher to teach is documented, otherwise you might get a babysitter or security guard instead of a teacher, and then your right to education is being denied.

Lack of human rights was the cause of the civil war. Human rights were civil rights in the southern states in the last century. Human rights are women's rights in the southern and heartland states right now. Human rights must be supported at the federal level, but this does not mean nor require funding state infrastructure.

Set infrastructure standards at the federal level and let states tax and manage their own infrastructure. Then the states have a clear picture of their situation. For example, several states may not be able to pay for teachers nor infrastructure. They must raise more revenue to do so. This makes the state financially undesirable. This is an accurate status, the citizens of those states must be aware of this, only then will they be honest about their situation.

This doesn't mean the wealthy states won't help them or not, it means they are not entitled to the tax revenue of wealthy states. It is up to a state to create an environment which incentivizes economic growth. Currently, many states do not do not have enough economic growth. This is because of their environment, which is social and economic, not weather, though weather must be a consideration in the design of economic growth. For example, a state with severe winters would have to have a different approach than a sun belt state. Many states are more focused upon denying human rights than economic growth, which will have a severe price.

This can be seen in health care, where care is limited in low population states. While people in these states are very unhappy with this, the people they elect are not interested in correction. You would think if this was such a big issue, they would elect other people, but they do not. Anecdotally, they complain about people they don't like causing their problems and do nothing to solve their own problems or their problems would be solved.

Term of Office

Term of office causes inequity and there can be a standard term for all offices. Four year terms would appear to work better than the variety of terms we have, but this could be another term but 2 years is too short. This would include Supreme

To Stop Extinction

Court justices. There should be no lifetime appointments, this is not a kingdom.

Simple Tax

The concept of Simple Tax is that a good portion of legislative time and energy is spent on deciding how much tax is collected, who pays that tax, and what to do with that tax money.

These activities are unnecessary and basically, distraction. Distraction enables dishonesty.

Currently, the main forms of tax collection are:

1.   Personal Income Tax

2.   Corporate Income Tax

3.   Property Tax

4.   Sales Tax

5.   Gas Tax

6.   Other Taxes.   These are typically taxes imposed by regulatory agencies, such as communications and utilities.

Currently , the main governments which collect these taxes are:

To Stop Extinction

1.　　Federal

2.　　State

3.　　County

4.　　City

To solve this mess, we use a Simple Tax. This simple tax is singular, so includes all taxes. This will be a large amount. There is good purpose to knowing exactly how much of your time in the form of money goes for maintaining the country, state, county, and city.

Simple Tax can be collected through a percentage of business bank deposits. The percentage of taxes collected can depend on the size of business. The larger the business, the larger the percentage. The purpose of this is that small businesses are stimulated.

A business should have a designated account where all receipts are deposited. A percentage of these deposits are taken as tax. The percentage of tax will be adjusted annually based on company annual sales.

The company could designate this tax as an addition to sales price. As a business owner, this type of tax added to a sale is inconsequential- it is just a part of a quotation and is not adjustable by the buyer or seller. An example is provided in a table below, values are example only and not accurate.

This table can be easily adjusted according to actual budgets. I seem to remember that a national sales tax would have to be double the values I have listed, but this is based on the actual cost of your governments from a recent year.

Sales	Fed.	State	County	City	Total
100,000	5%	1.0%	0.10%	0.10%	6%
1 million	10%	2.0%	0.20%	0.20%	12%
10 million	12%	2.4%	0.24%	0.24%	15%
100 million	15%	3.0%	0.30%	0.30%	19%
1 billion	18%	3.6%	0.36%	0.36%	22%
10 billion	20%	4.0%	0.40%	0.40%	25%
100 billion	22%	4.4%	0.44%	0.44%	27%
1 trillion	25%	5.0%	0.50%	0.50%	31%

The benefit of this is that taxation is no longer an argument. One of the main distractions politicians use is the collection and use of taxes, and it is easy to significantly diminish their responsibility for this.

While large companies will want their percentage lowered, it should be obvious that any lobbying by a large company is for their own benefit. Lobbying by any company should be illegal.

If a state has to raise their percentage, it should be approved by the people in an election, not by the representatives vote.

Simple Farming

Americans are separated from a crucial fact. We have handled land to live upon and a basic home for $83 a month. What else do you need? You need food, utilities, clothing, and health care. That's about it for basic needs. So, farming is not recognized as the most important profession, and farmers certainly aren't paid that way. We would suggest that small farmers should be treated differently: farming should be treated as the most important profession.

A farmer should get a paycheck which should be somewhere in the middle of the 7-tier pay structure. So, for example, the average pay in America is a good level to start. The farmer would then get a profit from whatever the value of his success. Just delivering the expected crop is excellent work, thank you, my family won't go hungry. This bonus might be the excess crop. So, if a farm produces $100,000 in food, and has $50,000 in costs and the farmer got $50,000 in pay, it's break even. If the farm made an extra $10,000, so $110,000 in food, the farmer gets that $10,000. Farming should be profitable and viewed as a good career choice; it's how we survive.

The farmer should be given land to farm food upon. We have the land. His ability as a farmer insures his allocation of land. While we currently have a system of farms mortgaged to the maximum, this causes great stress for the farmer and should be corrected. Allocating the land of our country for food production is a good use of our land. If a farmer is using the land to create food, that's a good idea.

If a farmer is producing something which is not food, such as ornamental pumpkins or whatever, that is not food and so it is not included. But, for example, hay is feed for animals who are food. Bees make food possible. So, supply chain farming must be considered as food farming.

The allocation of land might start at 25 acres for someone who wants to be a farmer. For a farmer who has a production record, the land allocation might be 100 acres. Or perhaps it depends on crop, for wheat you might need more a lot land than tomatoes. But there should be a maximum allocation because we want mid-sized farms.

Having many farmers ensures our food supply comes from many sources and we all survive. These numbers are known by the farming community.

I would suggest that farmers present a model for how much land a farmer needs. However, this would be for family farms. So, there might be a limit on staff outside of harvest time. Perhaps a family farm employs five or ten people besides any family outside of harvest time.

If the farmer already has a mortgage on the land of the farm, I would suggest they be relieved of this dependent on their ability to produce.

A country and its citizens have the right to determine farming standards. This would have to be done with farmers. For example, organic farming and free-range farming cost more than other methods.

Because everyone has been giving all their money for a mortgage, people cannot spend a lot on food. However, with the relief of that expense, the food budget can grow. Food is how we continue living.

I suggest a cost for food can be standardized based on the method and comparing all farmers. For example, what does it cost to grow tomatoes? Then, a good farmer should be able to grow tomatoes and sell them for a certain price which cover his costs, his paycheck, and his bonus.

While it may be argued that this would minimize the innovation and cost cutting incentives, the important concept here is that farmers are important, and their product is mandatory for a country to survive. Basically, we want farms to be family-owned, if possible, efficiently run, and create good food with reasonable margins. What is so difficult about this? This is the agreement between the citizens of America and its farmers. Why would we want to be unfair and unreasonable for the ones who feed us? We directly benefit from their work.

So, for example, it might cost $50,000 to grow and harvest a tomato crop. This can be financed and paid back from the crop. With the farmers salary of $50,000, that's $100,000 total. The expect crop with pricing guidelines should be at least 10% more, so $110,000 expected sales. Whatever the sales are more than $100,000, the farmer gets as his bonus.

If the production yields less than $100,000 or whatever is projected, an analysis should be done. Are other farmers able to be more profitable? How do they do it?

To Stop Extinction

If a farmer is consistently unable to produce at levels other same crop farmers do over the course of five year, they may love farming, but it's not a good business for them.

So, a simple deal for farmers would be:

1.   Simple Land and Simple Home programs provide every citizen a home.

2.   A salary which is equal to the average American income.

3.   Free use of land to farm upon up to maximum acres a family can farm for their chosen crop, which includes acres left unplanted for rotation.

4.   Financing of expenses.

5.   Expected production standards set by farmers.

6.   Additional production or sales income profits the farmer.

7.   Pricing guidelines based on cost to produce with standard margins.

8.   Analysis of shortfalls and assistance to correct for the next year.

9.   Five years to prove yourself as a farmer.

Simple Food

In the previous section, we presented the value of Farming and Farmers as being unique and something which should be valued highly.

Food and food processing are part of this.

The understanding is that is something qualifies as a food has special status.

In the Advantagist thinking, that people need food makes it grounds for price-gouging, i.e., how do I get an advantage and benefit exponentially from the fact that people need food. But that food can be grown and processed on such a large scale makes this impossible.

For this reason, food should be considered differently than anything else. After all, if you have a bit of land and your home on it, you can survive with food and water.

So, the price of food should be calculated according to a formula. To make things easy, the first component is the income of those who work in the industry. We dealt with farmer's compensation in the Simple Farming section.

The food processing and distribution staff are paid normal salaries like any company, so this is taken care of with Simple Pay.

There is then the cost to process and prepare food, and cost to distribute food.

The cost to process and prepare food, though typically proprietary in process, can be presented as a cost.

The cost to distribute food is not unlike distribution of other products so that has a known basis.

The food processor then can calculate a processing cost, and overhead cost and a profit. As there are thousands of food processing companies, these costs can be determined.

The food processor would then be able to deliver at a constant cost, and able to present any changes in their costs which relate to a change in price. Therefore, prices for food products can be set, monitored and adjusted as needed.

Food, being the main requirement for survival, can have prices set while other industries do not need such controls.

Because innovation is used to lower costs and offer different products, this also happens with food. So, a price for a food may be set, but another company may figure out how to make a similar food for a lower cost, and their sales prices can be set accordingly.

While the purpose of price fixing is to limit inflation, the purpose of this price fixing is to guarantee profit. The reason for this is that we eat food to survive. If a company is in this business, people are counting on them to survive. We want such a company to make a stable profit without interruption, that is best for people. We are not saying that the company makes all information public. This is not needed. But for analysis and pricing, the information can be shared with a department which does this. There is no purpose to sharing information from one company with another.

We do this by establishing a profit margin based on current sales prices. In the complete budget for a food product, all the costs are documented. The process may be proprietary, but the cost can be public. If the costs to the food processor go up, the price charged can go up.

In this way, the supply of food requires an extra level of monitoring, but this protects the people from price gouging, and protects the food processing company from losing money on a product. Because the pricing is documented we can assure the food supply to all citizens, even though the cost components are not still proprietary to a company.

Whether or not their products sell is dependent on the food processing company having a good product for the price.

Simple Immigration

Some people are opposed to immigration, though they are descendants of immigrants. The truth is that there are other issues in this protest. America's great strength is that it is a country of immigrants, and these are the current citizens.

Immigration is a benefit to everyone, but this is not obvious to everyone, so the model for immigration is incorrect. Immigration should be obviously beneficial to everyone. This advantage has been taken from citizens. American citizens should be able to see a direct benefit to them from immigration, and the structure of the economy is the reason citizens do not get this benefit.

To change this, we look at where the benefit occurs. A benefit occurs to the business who gets immigrant staff so that they can operate their business. A benefit occurs to local businesses who sell to the immigrant staff. A benefit occurs to the entire economy as it can grow beyond the labor of existing citizens.

To Stop Extinction

To make this simple, we will classify people as citizens and those with a work visa.

Moving from work visa to citizen can have requirements, such as working for a number of years in the country and not being convicted of a serious crime.

In this country, there has been a transitional status which has been organized with green cards, but this has not been properly managed and is outdated. To correct this, I would suggest eliminating the green card program. People with green cards should be converted to citizens to eliminate the green card if they have worked enough years. If they have not worked enough years, they can have a work visa until they work the additional years needed to qualify to be a citizen. There should be little cost for to apply for citizenship, perhaps the same cost as getting driver's license.

There will be no permanent designation for transitional. Someone with a work visa who meets the requirements can apply for citizenship. When they pass the test and become a citizen, they are no longer in America on a work visa, they are a citizen.

Work visas should be a managed program. This means that anyone wanting to come to America can apply at the American embassy in their country. If we have a job for them, they can be given a work visa and brought to America. As they don't have a place to stay, dormitories should be provided until they can afford and obtain a residence. The easier we make immigration, the larger our economy can grow and the more we benefit from immigration. A large part of the world would like to have what Americans have. We can enable this and benefit from it.

If there is no embassy in their country, they can go to a country where there is an embassy.

If people show up at the border, they can be processed similarly. So, this would mean the borders would have the equivalent of embassies.

If the USA does not have jobs, no work visas are needed at that moment. This is handled in the section on Simple Jobs.

To get employed, you must have a work visa. The work visa program would have to be strongly enforced and secure just like passports and driver's licenses and any legal identification.

We would not suggest political asylum. Most countries do not have human rights, so it can be assumed that everyone needs political asylum outside of first world countries with human rights.

For employers, there would have to be an employment department which provides workers. Every state has such a department, so it should be determined that all jobs pass through these departments. Currently, we apply for jobs online. It is a simple step that these jobs are registered with a state department. This registration and tracking can be automated.

If a job opening is open to immigrants, then immigrants with a work visa are processed this way. In this way, all immigrants with a work visa are registered. There are no new immigrants looking for jobs without work visas. The first job must be administrated.

After the first job, the immigrant with the work visa can obtain employment like any other person in America. This eliminates the idea that undocumented people are invading the country.

For employers, they would have to check the validity of the work visa to hire an immigrant. This can be automated online so that a photo and history is available. Security for this, just like driver's licenses and passports, is important. So, this level of security would have to be handled like government security clearances. This is because there will be great value to this work visa document outside the country.

Because some Americans still would not see a benefit, the benefit should be more direct, documented, and available. This is financial. As people with work visas are not eligible for social security and unemployment insurance, their incomes should not be subject to these taxes.

Their income tax should be a standard, fixed rate is taken out when then are paid. For example, this might be 25%. In addition, the employer would have an additional tax on the wages, such as 25%. This surtax for employing immigrants on work visas provides an incentive to employers to hire citizens.

So, if a job is paying $10 an hour, the citizen might take home 80% or $8 an hour if income tax is not included in this calculation but Social Security is included, simply because we are suggesting in Simple Tax that there be no personal income tax.

The immigrant would get $7.50 but the 25% tax would go to local taxes. In addition, the employer would be charged 25% or $2.50 an hour, so $5 an hour would go to local taxes. Immigration then directly benefits citizens, and immigrants get opportunity and safety. This provides an incentive to cities and counties to bring industry to their domain which requires more labor than is available locally. Cities and counties will then see immigration as what it is: a way to grow an economy and pay for public costs.

Instead of the money going to federal government or state government, the money would go to the city if the business is within a city, and to the county if the business is not within city boundaries in unincorporated areas of the county.

The totals of these contributions by immigrants to the local tax base can be reported publicly monthly. So, every month on the news it would be reported how much immigrants contributed to the city and county taxes. It would not be hard to determine how much immigrants spent of their paychecks in local businesses. For example, if you record all money sent abroad by immigrants, the remainder of their income was spent in this country. So, the public report for might be that immigrant contributions were $1 million to county taxes and immigrants spent $2 million locally in the last month. Properly managed, it may be that immigrants provide payment for the majority of county expenses. Properly managed in this case would mean that the county would provide incentive for businesses with immigrant jobs to locate in their county. Such incentives would not affect payroll tax liability which is set at the state and federal levels, but other incentives could be provided.

The amounts can be regulated, 25% from the immigrant and 25% from the employer was used in this example. The higher the number, the less conflict occurs from citizens. How high do these taxes have to be so that 75% of citizens agree it's a good thing? That determination will provide a good level. By the time an immigrant is eligible for citizenship, it is likely they have contributed more tax to the country than most citizens. They have earned citizenship.

Because we use English as our language, everyone who is in the country should attend English classes until they can converse successfully in English. For those over the age of 55, they have limited ability to learn a new language but should still attend classes, they just learn at a slower pace. If it helps, English can be made the national language. As Europe shows, having multiple active languages in a country is not debilitating, it is part of diversity.

Simple Vote

With Simple Government, we suggested a model where every citizen is only 1 or 2 people removed from the person in government. Every citizen would then can contact indirectly or contact the representative directly.

The representatives at the city, county, state, and federal levels will write the laws. These representatives can be selected by election or through neighborhood caucuses and then city or county caucuses. The role of government representatives is not to have the power, it is to administrate the funding the citizens approve.

We suggest that the citizens decide on funding the laws which removes that power from representatives. The citizens can also vote on what laws they want.

To enable this, we would suggest standard voting places which are regulated like any government function. These can be voting offices and could be integrated to something like the DMV or schools. Voting offices can be staffed by citizens as is done now. This would enable monthly voting if needed. And it would enable voting at any time. For example, the voting department could be open 24 hours a day for one week a month, or business hours a few days a week, off-hours a couple days a week, and one weekend a month. Hours can be flexible enough that everyone can go vote without difficulty. There can be a benefit for voting. This could be a direct payment in cash when you vote or any other method of benefit. My European acquaintances say they get about $25 to vote. It may not be important to some people to vote, and with our current American political system I don't blame them for apathy. But it is important to establish a culture of voting because that is a culture of human rights. It is important, it is worth focusing upon.

The voting for city, county, state and federal could then not be for just representatives, but for funding. The funding can be broken into departments, or purposes. What is important is that the breakdown on allocations be consolidated.

This means that there are only perhaps 25 categories on the voting. There could be a secondary breakdown, so that each of the 25 categories has a list of up to 25 allocations of that funding. Funding voting could be optional at the secondary level. That way, if someone is very concerned about such funding, they can have a vote on it. Otherwise, primary funding is probably good enough.

It would be up to the representative to break government funding into 25 departments or less. The purpose of the funding should be stated on the ballot. For example, every expense more than 5% of the department total should be stated. Citizens have a right to know how the money for a department is spent. That might include salaries, facilities, supplies, contracts, etc. If contracts are large, the ballot or supporting documents could state what type and size of contracts.

At the Federal level, what are the categories that are important? This is the challenge for lawmakers: to organize government and funding into categories that make sense to people and people can vote upon. This is important because it gives people the power. This is avoided because politicians want the power. If you are a politician and believe yourself to be a supporter of human rights, then support these human rights of Simple Government and Simple Vote in whatever form the citizens decide upon.

As funding is annual, people can place their votes for next year's funding during the previous year and potentially even change their votes if they change their minds.

If citizens want to change what percentage of tax is added to what size businesses, this can be done on the ballot.

Ballots should be simple and transparent. This can be a legal test which is applied. To get approval for a ballot, a representative group of citizens would have to approve a ballot for simplicity and transparency. If the representatives cannot provide such a ballot, then a group of citizens would point out the problems with the ballot.

Funding voting could be to increase or decrease funding for a department of the government, with a percentage choice. So defense spending might be $500 billion for last year. The ballot question would be do you want to increase or decrease defense funding. The ballot could offer a choice of percentage such as 1%, 2%, 3% or even 5%, and what that dollar amount would be. This can be done for every department. Citizens would have no reason to complain about government spending, they decided it.

Simple Tax government funding could be the same, with adjustable percentages for different sizes of businesses. These taxes do not come out of the company, they are added like sales tax to a sale. The larger the company, the larger the margin they work upon, that's why they make so much money, and that's up to customers. So, adding tax is not a deterrent to business, it's a normal part of business.

The concepts of Simple Vote are what is important. The details are up to the citizens.

The concepts of Simple Vote are:

1.   It's easy to vote. There is a regular polling place which has hours which make it easy for all citizens to vote. Voting would include mail-in ballots. It could be that a state goes entirely to mail-in ballots.

2.   Citizens have an adequate voting period to vote. Instead of a Tuesday in November, the voting period could include all of October. With a month to vote, everyone can participate.

3.   Establish a culture of voting. Citizens should have incentive to vote. This could be cash or a reduction on a utility bill, for example. The incentive should be significant enough that everyone votes.

4.   Citizens vote on government funding.

5.   Citizens vote on representatives

6.   Citizens vote on where taxes are collected and at percentages.

7.   Ballots are simple and transparent.

Simple Employment

The relationship model between employers and employees is illogical. The benefits are seen as held by employers and employees must comply. This does not support human rights. At the same time, the employer is held responsible for many things which are not the job. All of this needs a re-organization which gives employees a great quality of life and employers the work needed for wages they offer and that's it.

The interpretation of the Human Right to Work is handled on two issues in this document. The first we call Simple Employment.

Simple Employment means that everyone who wants a job should have a job. This creates the most productive economy. To assist in this, everyone who is not fully employed to their preference should be able to become employed. So, in A Definition of Human Rights, one of the rights is the right to work. The meaning of this is to right to have a job.

So, to achieve this, application and hiring methods will have to be changed.

Currently, there are many online job agencies. Employers post their jobs and applicants post their resume and the employers choose an applicant.

The flaw in this model is the understanding of the goal of making use of all people within our culture at their highest potential.

So, the most important part of a Jobs solution is to deal with everyone. Everyone should work. At the point when you cannot answer a phone, either physically or mentally, you should be fully retired. Until then, there is something you can do if you want to work.

There is a state Employment Development Department which manages unemployment and has a job board. The function of this department can be enhanced to assist in full employment.

Our country is offering us land to live upon, low-cost financing for our homes, utilities, and food. This creates an obligation of the person to their culture. This obligation is easily satisfied by work. While you think that you are receiving money for your time and this is true, the true importance is that you are participating in the culture's economy and therefore creating the culture.

81

If no one works, the culture will not exist. If everyone works, the culture will be most productive.

So, the understanding is that regardless of compensation, you are contributing to the culture in the form of work. If you want to live within a culture, you must contribute. We can call this your work obligation. Your obligation does not take money from your wages, like taxes, your obligation is met by your contribution to the culture in the form of work, as opposed to your contribution to your family by work within your home such as cleaning.

This is your contribution is to the GDP of the USA, do not diminish the value of this contribution. This is your contribution to the country which provides you with so much. Your contribution is not a portion of the money you receive as wages; your contribution is to the GDP of the country.

Now, with Simple Land, Simple Home, Simple Resources and Simple Food, you may only need to work 20 hours a month at a job to pay for your residence and food.

But some people have a hard time to find a job or not get hired or can't work full time. This immense resource is unused in our culture, with significant cost.

We can establish a way to correct this. For example, if someone is not hired within 90 days, they would be given a Priority Status for hiring. The Priority Status would signify that employment of this person has not taken place quickly and so they are moved to the front of the line.

There may be a significant reason why finding employment is challenging for this person. The understanding is that there is benefit to our culture and economy for everyone to have employment. The process is to assist in gaining employment and to provide feedback why this has occurred.

The priority hiring status could use temporary employment with companies who need extra help. To facilitate this for employers, it could include part of the wages. So, a person with priority status receives half of their wages paid from the government for a short period, perhaps 10 to 30 days of labor.

If a company does want to participate in this program, that should be acceptable and the company can pay a significant fine, such as 5% of their total labor cost for the year, to opt out of the full employment program. This cost is like unemployment, the need for which can be diminished significantly. If such companies exist, they could provide the wage compensation for other companies who do help us achieve full employment.

For companies who want to help everyone get employed, the total number of priority status candidates in a county can create a percentage of the workforce, and any company then becomes a percentage of that. For example, there might be 20,000 jobs in a county, there might be 1000 priority status candidates in a year, that's one of twenty. A company might employ 20 people. During that year, the company would do its part by taking one of the priority status candidates for a temporary period if the candidate applied for a job at the company.

If working temporary positions, there may be employment at more than one company. It would be understood that the employment is temporary. At the end of the employment, the employer could fill out a simple, anonymous review which includes productivity, quality, qualifications, attitude and ability to work with others, etc. Specifically, if the person would not be considered for permanent employment, what is the reason?

This review would enable a person to understand why they have not been hired. Any one or two reviews could be dismissed, but if someone has an issue which is repeated by several employers, then the issue could be determined. For example, if your productivity, quality or qualifications are at issue multiple times, this exposes the issue.

While most people like to be lazy now and then or on their time off, people don't like to be seen as lazy or not doing their part. So, to use all our human resources as a culture requires a different process than we have had. Currently, there are estimates that only about 60% of our labor force is used, and we see that the percentage is lower. Perhaps more than half of our human ability is not used. This is negative for self-esteem and creates economic hardship with whatever ramifications to our culture these problems entail.

While some may assert these people are to blame, we see that they need to be brought into the workforce in a supportive way. It is to everyone's benefit that everyone else is employed to the level they can choose and can handle.

Simple Working Relationships

The second part of the Human Right to Work presented in this document has to do with the working relationship between an employer and an employee. The naming of this as employer and employee would empower people more if the employer was understood as a company and the employee becomes a contractor. While this status has been subject to abuse in the past, we are going to show you how we convert this to advantage for both sides.

Because contractors do not rely on a company for Simple System benefits, contracting may have been seen as a company not honoring its obligations to staff in the past. However, these obligations are eliminated in this model. There should be no advantage to employer provided benefits, these benefits should be available to everyone. The benefit to humans is that you get all benefits without regard to employment, so you don't have to stay at a job because of the benefits.

The benefit to a company is they are not a benefits provider; their costs and obligations are reduced significantly.

As well, because humans have had a significant responsibility for paying mortgage interest, they could not go without pay for even a day, and this created a great obligation for companies for paying for time off, holidays, vacations, etc. This obligation is eliminated if you are not spending half your income on mortgage interest.

The transition for contractors is to determine their own work schedule through coming to agreement with a company.

The employer has the ultimate control for a contractor, which is to offer a contract or not. Outside of discrimination, there is no recourse for a contractor who does not get awarded a contract.

Currently a company has the right to set the standard work week, and typically does at 40, but there are many employments out there that stipulate 50-hour, 55-hour and 60-hour work weeks. This is unethical and should be illegal. This problem is easily solved with contractor status because a contractor says when they can get a project or task done.

Many companies prefer to have someone at the same job, week in, week out until all the life is squeezed out of them. There should be no minimum hours per week for employment, this should be the irrevocable right of the employee. In other words, it should be illegal for an employer to ask how many hours an employee will work.

An agreement between the employee and employer can be made, but the employee should be able to set the schedule they are available. So, if you like to work 20 hours a week, 3 weeks a month, 9 months a year, that should be just an honest statement. An employer might say they want people to work 40 hours a week. That can be made illegal for violating a person's human right to work the schedule they want. The employer can offer a contract with a maximum hours per week, but the minimum hours per week should be up to the contactor. To be clear, an employer can hire more contractors if they have more work.

An employer can hire as many people as they want to get as many hours as they need. There are no benefits obligations, no HR, no time off, no holidays. It is a contract. So, a person is offering to contract so many hours on a certain schedule. As a contractor, I can say that companies don't mind what days and hours you work, they are looking for a task to be completed. The reason they don't mind is that they only pay for the work, not your health care, time off, HR management, etc.

An employer can require production and quality, and if the employee does not meet the employer's standards, the company can stop the employment. There should be no reasons needed for dismissing an employee, if the employer deems the employee does not meet their standards for any reason, they can be terminated. The contract can be terminated, or more commonly, the contract is not renewed.

The exception to this is discrimination. For example, the employee is from Pluto and asserts that the employer discriminates against people from Pluto. However, the employer has another Plutonian employed, as well as a Saturnian and a Martian. So, the assertion of discrimination on the basis of race is not valid. A more obvious reason would be that the employer doesn't like how you did the job, that is enough grounds for termination. However, if the employer says they don't like people from Pluto and has no employees from Pluto, that may be discrimination.

The reason this is explained here is that legal protections for employers and employees are not logical in some agreements. So a company asking for things which are against employment laws would not make the law bypassed, it would make the employer liable for a significant fine. An employer can hire as many contractors as they need, they don't need to make demands on contractors. Now, many contractors will want to get wealthy by working 40, 50 and 60 hours a week. Or they just enjoy working. But that is their choice.

These contractor rights would be irrevocable. Any signed agreement stating rules contrary to these employer and employee rights are not legitimate nor recognized. Basically, you can't sign away your rights, but employers can be fined significantly just for trying to take away your rights, for writing illegal contracts which do not support your human rights. Employers still can't discriminate on the basis of race, sex, etc. The new addition to the list of discriminations would be discrimination for contractors choice of work schedule.

For example, if people average 30 hours a week nationwide, and a company has everyone working 60 hours a week and someone's contract is terminated because they sign up for less than 60 hours a week offered, that's discrimination. The contractor doesn't have to sue, it's a criminal offense.

It can be challenging for an employer to find the right staff. To enable people to work a schedule they want requires this additional effort of hiring more staff from employers because many contractors don't want to work 40 and 50 hour work weeks. On the other side, the employer is relieved of significant burdens such as providing HR, benefits, time off and employing people who do not meet their requirements.

So, how this could work is that a company offers you a contract of up to 20,30,40,50,60 hours a week which could be continuous until changed. You take how much you want. They offer 40 hours a week, you may sign up for shifts which total 30 hours a week.

A company has a right to know your schedule a week or two in advance, that is reasonable. If you can let them know a couple months schedule, even better. If you repeatedly don't honor your commitments, they can remedy this by not offering another contract, or terminating a contract for non-performance.

You cannot have a place in a company where the owner doesn't want you there. People should find employment where the company appreciates them. That will make them much happier in their employment. Full employment is the goal. Which company, which job and what contract rate is to be determined.

If the employer has a job, there should be several people who can do that job, and the available work can be signed up for. If that doesn't fill the employer's schedule, then the employer is paying too little, the wage they are offering does not motivate anyone to take the job.

The reason for allowing an employee to work whatever schedule they want is quality of life. The employee's quality of life must be respected. Lack of quality of life can cause dis-satisfaction, anger, frustration, sadness, hopelessness.

A great part of this dis-satisfaction is the requirement of showing up every day, every week, every month. This is why people look forward to retirement so much. They don't always admit it, but many people do not actually like their job.

Here's how to tell if you like your job. Would you enjoy your job if it did not pay? If you would do your job even if it did not pay, you like your job. Of course you work for money, so that is just a rhetorical question.

Your enjoyment of your job could be high or low or in-between. This is a grey scale, you may like your job more than any other job you see, so it is your choice of jobs. You like your job enough to work for less, even though you don't have to. For example, if you find yourself working more than 40 hours when you are paid for 40-hours, you like your job or at least you get satisfaction from doing your job properly.

But for people who do not like their job so much, getting away from your job dramatically improves your quality of life. So, perhaps you want to work every other week or every other month or every other season- these schedules would be about 1000 hours a year.

You may find that if you work every other month, your job doesn't bother you that much. In this case, you don't have to dream of retirement, you can partially retire for the rest of your life starting now. Perhaps you work 20 hours every other week, but then you want a break and take two months off. That's quality of life.

For people in the current enslavement culture, they must work 40 hours a week every week to pay the mortgage, which is simply interest which somehow ends up with the wealthiest 1%. The 1% just buy assets with it or stick it away, so basically their nest egg gets bigger with every week you work.   This is not a good thing, and it is unnecessary.

Simple Land, Simple Home, Simple Food changes everything.   Simple Jobs in two aspects for full employment and working relationship completes the first phase of concepts.

Companies will simply have to have double the number of employees if people work half as much.

Simple Retirement

As you age, you may not be able to work the 360 hours a year to satisfy your contribution to the country. This will be from physical disability or mental disability.

In the case of physical disability, it should be determined what physical tasks the person is capable of and then employment should be found accordingly.

In the case of mental disability, the same applies.

If someone is incapable of work, as happens for everyone, then their retirement would cover their minimum hours and pay needed.

So, rather than a fixed retirement, a progressive retirement should be planned for.

For example, let's say your financial obligations are Simple Home, Simple Food and Simple Health. Let's say, according to our example, this is $8400 per year.

At age 55, we might see a reduction in labor to 80%.

At age 60, 70%.

At age 65, 60%.

At age 70, 40%.

At age 75, 20%.

The culture would provide compensation for Simple Home, Simple Food and Simple Health accordingly, as well as an additional percentage commiserate with the person's average amount of work over their work history.

If the person can work more and wants to work, that's fine.

After age 75, the workload can be reduced to whatever the person can handle if anything.

The details provided for this model are limited but can be detailed if such a program is implemented.

Simple Natural Resources

All resources of a country belong to all citizens of the country. That these have been sold is inappropriate and should be corrected. This does not mean that any assets should be seized. Re-distribution of wealth is never needed or a good precedent.

Assets such as water rights, oil, gas, coal, minerals, elements, geo-thermal, solar, wind and any other natural resources have a value. If these assets are owned by a company or individual, that asset has a determinable value and should be purchased back at their value from whoever has obtained these assets. This can be done through something like eminent domain for resources.

After that, there can be contracts to pump or mine the asset and contracts to process the assets as is needed. So an oil company or mining company becomes a contractor and can build their profit into their bids.

The assets can be sold at cost to citizens. This would stabilize prices, such as gas prices.

If there is surplus or demand for a resource such as a mineral or gas, people can vote to sell this surplus on the open market or to other countries.

Simple Law

The concept of Simple Law is that laws are simple. So, the legal cartel in America utilizes a version of language which can be called legalese for this presentation.

Legalese uses precise, elaborate phrasing to include all possible events with regards to a resolution.

The Simple Law is a common language version.

While legalese may have developed to provide clarity through thorough resolution, the result in our culture is that legalese is part of providing rule of law.

At the same time, this state provides advantage to lawyers. You must have lawyers create legal documents and handle situations where interpretation takes place.

When you go to a lawyer with a legal document which may be any number of pages, the lawyers review the document and may tell you, for example, "it says you can't commit fraud against the company."

This legal structure is cumbersome without reason when simplicity is the rationale for system design.

A legal statement can be "You can't commit fraud against this company." The legalese can follow with whatever detail is legally appropriate, with any number of pages.

But the Simple Law legal statement is: You cannot commit fraud against this company, that is the law. The legalese is generated from a complete disclosure of details but is derivative of the Simple Law. The simple explanation your lawyer gives you is the law; the legalese is the description of details.

This means that you will be able to read the legal agreements you sign. A simple standard would be that a legal statement would have to be 25 words or less in common language.

The test for this can be to give the legal statement to a panel of people who are a cross-section of the population and ask them what the Simple Law legal statement means. If the Simple Law legal statement is understood by most, it's good.

So, there may have to be several Simple Law legal statements at the start of a Terms and Conditions agreement. But reading ten simple legal statements can be done and then you know what you are signing.

This applies to all laws. This includes municipal laws such as cities and counties, to state and federal laws. The law can be that each law must have a simple legal statement as it's description and the legalese can be at the end.

But the point is that the simple statement is the law, the legalese is just a thorough description of the simple law.

Because a simple legal statement will be limited in length, there may need to be any number of statements in a law.

State and federal laws should have to be approved by a panel of citizens based on whether the simple law is easy to understand.

If a proposed federal law has too many simple legal statements, for example, twenty, then the panel can tell the legislators to go back and come up with two laws which have ten statements each. In other words, if a law takes more than ten statements of 25 words or less, it's no longer a Simple Law.

Jurisdictions can do this immediately. To make it simple, only elect people who agree to go through all the laws of the jurisdiction and convert them to Simple Law, and only make Simple Laws in the future.

This will take back citizens' power from the legal cartel. You can write a simple document which has legal power. The simple legal statement is legal, the legalese would only be the thorough interpretation of the statement with all details.

In addition, complex legal interpretation can be made simple. For example, there can be a law which says, "Fraud means you intend to..." and then the violations can follow, such as cheat, steal, misrepresent facts, conceal important information, etc. You get 25 words. A culture could be more tolerant and decide 50 words maximum works better, or 35 words. These are details which people can determine if they work together.

The point is most people have a general understanding of fraud, agreeing to not commit fraud does not take ten pages of legalese, it can be summed up in a simple legal statement, "I will not commit fraud against this company." The legal definition of fraud is then the 25 or 50 word statement, and so using the word fraud means that

To Stop Extinction

25 word definition will be applied. Anyone who works around this simple law has the intention to commit fraud, and maybe does commit fraud.

Part 2: A Plan

In The 5000 Year Message, we are given the assembled version of a guide to being human delivered over the last 5000 years.

In A Definition of Human Rights, we defined human rights from an off-world perspective.

In Part 1 of this book, we provided examples of Simple Systems which are based on the definitions of human rights.

In Part 2 of this book, we provide a plan for implementation of the Simple Systems. This implementation provides significatant improvement of our chances of stopping extinction.

Plan Overview

In this part of the book, we will present a plan to stop extinction.

First, the obvious question: why don't Extra-Terrestrials or a divine being step into save us.

Next, to stop extinction we present 7 Words. 7 Words is a 3-step guide for you to determine if you are on the path to stop extinction.

To do your bit, we present Activation. We call doing what you can do Activation. What this plan needs from you is very small, you can handle it between dinner and sitting down to look at your feed, watch TV, or get on your computer. This is how you, the one reading this, stop extinction, or not. We don't think you will get a better offer than 10 minutes once a month to stop your extinction.

We discuss the building of the Communications Bridge, the so-called Portal.

We present Planetary Equalization which is needed to economically equalize the countries of the planet.

We present Ending Conflict. This is an overview of how we resolve conflict off-world and hope to provide this service to earth to resolve conflicts. When you have the truth, conflicts can be resolved or not. This identifies who wants the conflict resolved, meaning they can be part of stopping extinction. And it identifies who does not want the conflict resolved now.

We present A Stable Economy. This enables us to have a stable economy so that focus is removed from this issue. Basically, if you don't have to be concerned with an issue every day of your life, it's not a problem. For example, most people don't worry everyday if the light switch is going to work in the bathroom.

We present Supersession. Supersession is how we stop extinction in the rest of the world.

We present the offer for Off-World Technology. If we can activate people or assemble resources or both, we can bring the tech. If we are hell bent on extinction, tech won't help anyway. The exception is the Communications Bridge, the portal to Off-

World, the real world. With this technology we can obtain truth, and the truth always has an impact.

With all this information, we present a five step Launch. Our presentation in these 3 books started as more than 50 transmissions, so we can't do 50 things at once, but all of them must be addressed for all humans to have wealth and security and for us to stop extinction.

Extra-Terrestrial or Divine Intervention

The most obvious solution to the issue of humans would be intervention from the off-world community.

For some people, discussion of extra-terrestrials is grounds for lacking credibility and scorn. This subject is sometimes cause for suggestion of mental problems and hallucinations, which is tolerated by others rather than being honest. The same is true for discussion of divine or celestial beings or beings who do not have physical bodies.

This assertion of lack of credibility is probably close to 100% true for people who have to maintain a public credibility, such as politicians, public personalities and journalists.

These attitudes and assertions are based on dishonesty and fear. These people have an advantage and they feel that making admissions may cost them their advantage. They are concerned for their survival, utilizing the instinct to survive as the reason for being dishonest. It is true that some people just do not care, and this is also indicative of a fear of losing advantage. In other words, there is no advantage given and possible loss of advantage to be honest. In their case, honesty would be they don't care about these issues, they only care about maintaining their advantage.

We come from a different place, we come from that place where these beings are part of the community. Certainly, the first question which all of these people would assert is, "where is the proof."

While we did not expect this response from the off-world community, the response has been that they will provide proof on your terms. Because we understand the nature of proof to humans, proof is provided for an individual; this proof is provided to you, personally. We provide detail about this in the section about the Communication Bridge.

So, in this section, we will discuss intervention to stop human extinction by extra-terrestrials and divine beings who are members of the off-world community.

At present, we are aware for no plan for a divine intervention event such as happened 2000 years ago through Jesus. This doesn't mean we are aware of every projection, so some projections include a divine intervention event. But these events are large plans with thousands working on them off-world. So, there would not be just a bunch of work going on off-world, there would be people talking about it on earth as well. I don't see this. The conclusion is that stopping extinction is up to humans to change perspective. The current human perspective is to live by the instinct to survive, fight to survive and get ahead without concern for others. Our perspective must change to understanding that everyone must work together to survive .

In the movie The Day the Earth Stood Still this was decently depicted showing the trauma, chaos, and resistance such an extra-terrestrial intervention would cause. The movie depicted the plan as killing all humans. Killing humans is not the plan. Extra-terrestrial movies usually have this theme, that is not how they work, that is how humans work. Aliens don't have to destroy humans; humans are destroying each other right now all by themselves. The best plans are humans not killing each other nor dying by destruction of the planet.

But the real reason is not the trauma such an intervention would cause. Though none of you remember such events, an intervention occurred a long time ago. The intervention worked well, but post-intervention the humans almost destroyed the planet. Basically, human nature and perspective had not changed.

This time, the goal is to expose that human nature must change and this change is by a conscious decision by humans. To date, humans have not been able to make such a change. Humans know the difference between right and wrong but use different motivations to choose their actions.

So, an extra-terrestrial intervention is not the plan. There are many extra-terrestrial species who are aware of our impending extinction. There are a few extra-terrestrial species who are actively involved.

Some, like the greys, believe that humans are a primitive species so their plan is to develop and release a hybrid human which is not so volatile at the point when humans go extinct. Their plan is not to save humans, but to save the earth and present a new species. This new species will have less free will and some telepathy. This will diminish the emotional amplification of humans as well as our inclination to survive at the cost of others.

111

In comparison to our culture, this will diminish the focus on getting ahead and leaving others behind. The greys have mastered some of the universal technologies such as ensoulment, so therefore their recovered bodies have no digestive system, they are short term ensoulments. But development of a hybrid species is not so easy, and this project does not have much support off-world.

Other extra-terrestrials are available, supportive to some extent and willing to help. However, if we are destroying each other, for them there is no point in taking sides.

While in America we like to think we are the good guys, the test of this off-world is support of human rights for all people. The off-world community would like to see this support of human rights world-wide, but we don't even support human rights for the people in our country. So, this is the starting point for Americans, and a decent tool is the 7 Words program. It is within our power to be the good guys, please start now.

Currently, we can't even end conflict between ourselves, so therefore a part of the plan in this section of the book is Ending Conflict. While all the politicians, statesmen and pundits have not ended conflict, our perspective off-world is honest: they don't know how, haven't tried, or don't want to end conflict. Some want to increase conflict for their own reasons. They haven't tried is the conclusion because though some may say they want to end conflict, what they really want is to get the other side to go along with what they want. As can be seen by the result, this is not how you end conflict.

Some conflicts cannot be ended because one side wants to destroy or conquer the other side. We are not referring to those conflicts, which we can identify.

Most conflicts can be ended. Basically, each side gets a lot of the good things they want for themselves, but not the vengeance they want imposed upon others.

Vengeance is above our pay grade, that's taken care of by another department, and continues to be reconciled in another place and time.

You may ask why human rights, ending conflicts and vengeance are of concern to extra-terrestrials. How can we have association with other species when we can't even handle associations with each other?

So, all of this is what the supportive extra-terrestrials see. It doesn't mean they won't step in, but if they have not made their presence known, it means it is not the right time yet.

We can facilitate these extra-terrestrial relationships, even with the greys. When I say "we", I include my off-world contacts. There is no vacuum off-world, I can't do something that is invisible to others, and if they want the same thing, a resonance exists which connects all of us of like mind.

We interact with these ET's all the time off-world. Last time I requested a meeting off-world with the greys they responded same day and that was this year. I was just checking; I don't really like them. If I play the grey card, we must be ready, like really ready because our agenda is not their agenda. I would prefer another ET species over greys.

We see a big difference between being on earth and off-world, greys don't see this difference so much. I know these guys. You make contact off-world, and they could decide to visit you on earth, and they truly do not care what your feelings are on the issue. They don't take offense at my emotions of liking them or not, they see our emotions as curious and primitive.

It's not like I'm I have enormous credibility with these guys, it's more like, "why is that human who used to be our pet calling?" I make fun of them, but the truth is that they are not malicious, they just see that we are not stepping up.

They see we are destroying the planet and instead of stopping, we are busy quibbling amongst ourselves. In the movies, when the countdown to destruction starts, the hero is working to stop it even if it kills them. In our reality, we are arguing over who is wearing the best outfit or who is in charge. You know the countdown to destruction has started, right?

I know for many humans there are unanswered questions: do ETs exist, have they been on earth in the past, what do they want, etc. I can answer all these FAQ anytime if that will help. We can get proof on your terms. We have bigger fish to fry.

So far, people are still focused on their daily grind. So, the next step in extra-terrestrial relationships is for you personally to look up and make some decisions on the concepts in these books. You can't decide for anyone else, you can only make your choices, and that would be great.

I suppose some will want to know if we can facilitate meetings with extra-terrestrials. Typically, these people want such meetings on their terms, which is not of interest to these species. Second, do they want to meet you? As soon as you ask for a meeting, they will go to the Archives and determine your motive. Then they will look at your thoughts and actions. While the archive, the records of truth have privacy controls, if you are active in the world that is for all to see.

I meet and know them because I'm a dualist. I don't meet them on earth, that would be silly, they exist off-world and so do I some of the time, so there has to be a very good reason to meet on earth takes some doing and takes the risk of trauma and chaos. I meet them off-world. Remember every species is a member of the off-world community, so what is happening on earth has some management guidelines which most species follow unless they have a very good reason to do something else.

Off-World there is constant contact, we have many residents from many species. There are representatives of all the species in our neighborhood of the galaxy and some visitors from other neighborhoods as well. Some suggest that there may be fifty such species. There are many, I don't remember, and I don't interact with that many and I don't think of them as alien so much as humans do. There are several species who are present and active in off-world activities around earth, these are the ones from whom I can get different levels of help.

Generally, their attitude is that humans haven't grown up yet and many don't think we will. It's amazing to them that some humans think they can hurt other people to achieve something, or there is a real benefit to power and control over other humans. And I have to agree with them, that behavior is primitive and ignorant, but that doesn't mean humans can't grow beyond being stupid, that's what this project is about.

They must see it to believe it. Some are here just for that reason. They don't need us, they don't need our planet, they don't have malicious intent, they are visiting and meeting and participating. They each bring a unique perspective and experience, and this exposes the intent of the designer.

Every year which means constantly, the designer starts another species somewhere in the universe. A new species is a big project with lots of activity even though you start with single cell lifeforms, it must be designed to work in the conditions of the planet.

To Stop Extinction

The general parameters of life on that planet must be extrapolated a billion years to achieve complex eco-systems and species which can be ensouled.

Off-world, we have no specific access to that much information that is not related to earth. That will come later, and earth's available information is so much that we can't really get a handle on it. Most of the records that are available relate to humans. Most of the rest is about our neighborhood of the galaxy or general cosmology.

Every year, a species goes extinct. Some don't go extinct due to self-destruction, there are other reasons. But for species like humans, there's a likelihood of self-destruction, and it's our time.

This doesn't mean off-world they want extinction. The off-world does not want extinction, humans are causing their own extinction. 8 billion continue working towards this everyday thinking they are surviving another day, but ignoring that the days of survival will end. Perhaps adults will live out their days, but their children will not be able to survive.

You would think humans would want their children to survive. Facts show otherwise, at least not enough to do something about it. We already deal with these humans all the time off-world. At first, they are in denial, saying they didn't know or believe extinction was on the table. Soon enough they admit they were unable to overcome their emotions and beliefs prompting them to focus on their own survival.

Humans have free will. This most often means they are not interested in truth, they are focused upon proving what they believe to be true. One tale is no better than another to a human. For example, take yourself, are you interested in truth or does this seem just the rantings of another lunatic on earth?

Life on this planet was started a billion years ago or so. It's a billion year project, but what are you going to do if you have a trillion planets in the universe to work with? We live time a moment at a time. But what if you control time, it doesn't control you?

Anyway, extinction is very rare, and the ET species are arriving to see how this could happen. Most have never seen such an event like human extinction and will never see one again.

7 Words

With the book *The 5000 Year Message*, we are given a guide to being human by the designer. In about 25 words. It was started 5000 years ago and arrived this year for you. It is a way to help you understand your experience as a human.

You can say it's not possible, but it is.

You can say you don't believe it, but you will.

Now, from the same source, at the 11th hour, we are given maybe 7 words on how we each can save the world. In 3 small steps. That would be awesome if I could take credit for the 7 Words solution, but that would be presumptuous.

14 years ago, I told the story of a woman who did something unusual. And one day, I asked her why, and she said, "it's something beautiful...that I can do." She didn't feel she had anything to offer the world, but this was something beautiful that she could do.

Now it's your turn. On this foundation, we save the world. But it's not me, it's you. It's you who saves the world. With 3 small steps, maybe 7 words.

Our Foundation is that 7 words will save the world. If earth is saved from extinction, the concepts of these 7 words will be in the mindset whether this program is known or not known.

You can take these 3 small steps. At home, sitting at your kitchen table, you can do your bit to save the world. And all you must do is take 3 small steps...with your mind.

Don't make it more difficult than this because it's not. The rest will follow because it has no choice but to follow. You will be compelling because of 3 steps you have taken with your mind. You will be a magnet which draws balance to the world. Maybe not today or tomorrow, but over the course of the next decades.

You may think I'm just saying words, making stuff up. But in time, you will look back and know that you saved the world, because saving the world for you can only be what you can do. You can't do more than what you can do. You are not being asked to do more than you can do.

But you don't know what to do to save the world. You feel there is nothing you can do to save the world. But that's not true, you can do this to save the world.

My part is to tell you that you will look back and know someday that you did the right thing, and it did matter. It made all the difference, even though you couldn't see it at the time.

You don't have to see all of that, you just have to look at yourself and that's enough. Your task has always been to make you your best self. And this is how you can do it. And you can feel good about yourself for this reason. In you mind, you know that you did the right thing.

You will stumble, you're human, but if you give yourself a simple understanding, you will always be able to get back on your path. This is something beautiful that you can do. Right here, right now. And with this beauty you create, because you decided to do it, if you don't the part you would play will not be played.

You don't have to tell anyone that you have made this decision, but you can tell whomever you like.

Perhaps this is just a book, and these words are just a bit of ink on paper. But, perhaps, this is message sent to you personally.

You really want to, but the world is so filled with hurt, we stay where we are safe if we can find that place. And we all wonder, can't this world be better?

All that causes pain in the world has it's time and is over and turns to dust. But that which is real lasts. And you are here to do something real when it really matters.

Step 1: Be sincere.

Step 2: Be honest.

Step 3: Support human rights.

That's it. Seven words. Three steps. And you have done your part. What these steps mean to you will unfold as you live your life. In every interaction, you take 3 steps with your mind.

How can this save the world?

Because, if everyone does it, what problem still exists in the world? What is the problem which comes to your mind? Is it not solved for any group of people who take these steps?

And if you want a next step to solve the problem which comes to your mind, If you understand how that problems can be solved with a simple solution, then your decisions follow. So, 7 words are not the solution, 7 words are presented here as a way to understand a basis for making decisions before you think, speak and act.

But not everyone will do this.

Not today, but over time groups of people will, and they will come to act together. Every person who sees the problem that you see wants a simple solution. Like magnets drawn together, and magnets pushing away from those who don't want to save the world.

Some will be taking these 3 steps even if they never read these words, and they will save the world, because they will do what they can do, no more is asked and no more is required.

Step 1: Be Sincere

Being sincere means being authentic, by speaking your truth based on how you feel, what you think and believe. You don't have to add emotion because you feel that is the only way to be heard. If you act with sincerity, you already have more power than you may feel.

Step 2: Be Honest

Being honest does not mean saying bad things and things that hurt. It simply means not saying something false. Many different emotions from love and fear can generate reaction and response. If a response is hurtful and the truth is beautiful, then that response is not the entire story, it is part of the pain. You don't really want to be a purveyor of pain.

If the question violates you right to privacy, then you don't answer it with that reason: that is personal. Or simply: I don't have to answer that.

Being honest means telling the truth when it is important to tell the truth: when someone else is not telling the truth. The truth at that moment is: the other person is not telling the truth. You may not know what the truth is or may not be able to think of it at any given moment, all you have to know is that the truth is beautiful and the other person is only telling a half-truth or something which is false.

Step 3: Support Human Rights

Supporting human rights is the big challenge for many. We support our human rights, but can we support the human rights of others?

By supporting human rights of others, it is included that our human rights are supported, too. We support these human rights for everyone.

While so many claim their rights are violated, what rights are these?

These human rights are provided and explained in the book A Definition of Human Rights. To support human rights, you must know what human rights are, all your human rights. We have a list, it's just a list, but it's a pretty good list.

It doesn't matter where you are if you can shut out the world for a couple minutes. But maybe make a note of where you are, for this is where and when you decided to save the world. That's a big decision. For each step, you think about it for a few seconds, understand what it means, and make a decision in your mind. Whenever you don't know what to do, review your choices with the 3 steps as your understanding.

I will be sincere.

I will be honest.

I will support human rights.

That's it. You did it.

Activation

Most people must deal with the world. We must get to work in the morning. This is part of what they want to help us change. This is your quality of life tapping on your shoulder. You see, the two-stage concept of this projection is that by fixing stuff for humans, humans can fix stuff for earth. This is a bold wager, off-world, heads are shaking: if we give humans a better life, they will stop hurting each other and repair earth. Like we say, 30% chance on a good day.

And, as ridiculous as it sounds, they assert to me that all we must do is care. But in this case, caring means being sincere and honest and supporting human rights. It's not just "I care", it's "Because I care, I'm sincere and honest and I support human rights."

How does that work? There are a few little tasks you can do if you care, but they're not that big. Many of us could do these tasks while we sit at the kitchen table. Less than ten minutes, but even if you want to do more, it's less than hour a month while at home. If you choose to do something, it's ok even if you can only handle the smallest of somethings. Everyone is welcome, if you are human, you are needed.

Activation is the process of making change occur in the physical world, here on earth.

So, activation is the important step which sets change in motion. If a large enough group of people want something good, the change is initiated.

How to do this is mysterious to most people. Off-World, we see exactly how it takes place. Unfortunately, most of these activations are not for making the world a better place. So, we want to activate. We will do this for specific reasons at specific times with specific actions.

So, sign up with us so we can activate you when the time is right. We do not call to sell you something or talk you into something. We can text you or email you when an action is needed. We will provide you with what to do, which usually will not take more than ten minutes. You will not have to convince anyone of anything. It's that easy. Because we know how this works, we can make something happen if enough people sign up to allocate ten minutes of their time. We need about a million people to want to save the world. It takes place in small actions by you. No one will make you do something you don't want to do, that's not how we change the world.

We need a million and there are 8 billion on earth. So, we need one of ten thousand humans to give 5 minutes a month to save themselves and 10,000 more humans, people they don't know. I know, it's a hard sell, no takers yet.

Planetary Equalization

Planetary Equalization refers to economic equalization between the different countries on earth.

This is a relatively simple correction, however, the reason it has not been implemented is that the individual countries are controlled by people and groups who do not want equalization or perhaps no one understands the importance.

The purpose of equalization is to end conflict and use of energy for something which is unnecessary but serves the short term personal goals of people.

When we look at currencies, we are not looking at the correct asset.

The asset we should be looking at is time. Currency can then be understood to be a local valuation of time.

Every human has their time on earth, and they sell this time locally for a local currency.

In any two countries, a task takes a certain amount of time. This might be an hour of human time for a task. The value of that task is then converted to the local currency.

To equalize currencies, we start with time. If a task takes an hour, it results in a local value of one currency in a country, and results in another value of another currency in another country. The skill level of the task adjusts the local value in currency.

The comparative value of the currencies is determined in this way, separate from any trading value of the currencies which floats and is speculative.

When a product is imported or exported, it can be the option of the importing country to apply equalization cost to the imported item. This may be levied as a tariff or another title as is politically expedient, but this knowledge exists off-world as time-based equalization.

In this way, an item will cost the same to deliver from another country or be made in the same country it is sold.

This will normally apply to countries where the comparative currency has greater value. In practical terms, a first world country applies equalization to imports from third-world countries.

131

A third-world country does not apply equalization to imports which would be compensation to reduce the cost of the import.

Rather than viewing this as a penalty tariff, it can be seen as equalization, colloquially termed as leveling the playing field.

This has not been instituted in the USA because there are those who gain advantage from avoiding equalization using inciteful political rhetoric, and the penalty is paid by specific groups of Americans who cannot compete in an unbalanced environment.

Put simple, large groups of certain types of jobs went away in America because Advantagists or Elites don't care or don't understand about humans and human nature. More precisely, they do not care about other Americans. The accurate perspective for Advantagists is to understand they will not just lose their advantage, they could lose everything if they don't understand other humans are not like them. Don't expect other humans to be able to do what you have done. Be proud you can add value to the world.

The Elimination of Conflict

So, with conflict, there is an absence in the knowledge of objective truth and the perspective. The perspective could be an individual or a group of people, which we call a culture.

All the conflicts we have on earth, off-world we routinely solve. So, this concept is to bring that solution model to earth.

To resolve a conflict the first access takes place off-world. Most don't have conscious access to this dataset, so this is not possible, and for most there is the belief such an archive does not exist.

Then there are the normal privacy controls in place, so an individual must give permission before the archives can be viewed. This access enables determining the actual thinking and emotions of each of the parties.

At the start of the process, the parties are more concerned with their injuries of the past than a future. The future is unknown, the injuries of the past are known and perhaps indelible and profound.

On earth, the parties only expose what they must expose, the truth is camouflaged. If the individual is aware of their truth, they may keep it hidden. This may be due to embarrassment, it may be due to a concept that exposure does not benefit them, or many other perspectives. The truth is typically mostly emotional, but most of the time there is a historical basis which is not simply emotional response and reaction.

An individual may not even know the truth.

Beyond the emotion and goal based on these emotions, there is a truth. Now, if the truth is that one party seeks to kill, annihilate, conquer, or control the other party, there is no peaceful conflict resolution which satiates that truth.

Each party must want something for themselves or their side. And that wanting must be something besides destruction or control of the other side. They must want something. So, the next step is the identification of what each party wants for themselves.

The solution will then provide what the parties want for themselves, rather than negative action towards the other side. The desire for the negative action, the desire for the infliction of penalty, is not the solution.

In many conflicts, some asset is claimed by both sides. If both sides have validity to their claim, the resolution is some division and working relationship with regards to the asset.

Those who deal with negotiation will probably say this is oversimplified and will not work. My response is that we do this all the time with the same conflicts they have not resolved. We work out these resolutions at the same time their negotiations fail. In other words, there is a resolution Off-World which is acceptable to the parties but was not achieved on earth.

The reason is that access to truth provides the solution.

Often, upon realizing the postures of the parties to a conflict, the negotiators resign themselves to the initial presentation that an end to the conflict is not possible. Postures are not the only aspect to the conflict and the resolution.

What we see most of the time is that they negotiators have not ascertained what each side actually wants for themselves or their side.

When we look at conflict from off-world with access to the truth, we see that often the two sides are arguing about different things. They are wanting different things. Because they want something different, a resolution will involve each of them getting some part of what they want.

Now, there must be incentive as well. Each side sees their claim as their potential or temporary asset. So, if the assertion is just to settle for less than their potential or temporary asset, they will see themselves as getting nothing.

Additionally, the off-world negotiations are typically done with each party separately. The only meeting is the manifestation of the resolution, the formal agreement event.

Now, all these postures and back-and-forth attempts are probably well-known to negotiators. The missing element is the truth. Often, the negotiators have been told the truth or have discerned the truth, but the truth is not complete enough to provide resolution.

The truth in this case provides the understanding of whether a resolution can be achieved or not, and what that resolution might look like.

In some cases, we see that the third-party negotiators are the ones who do not want conflict resolution for their own reasons.

I understand that this seems a simplification, but if conflict exists, the parties have not done what has been done off-world for the situation already. This could be a conflict between family members or between countries.

Nevertheless, we are available to analyze any conflict, and provide relatively quick resolution where resolution is possible, but also define where parties to a conflict are not interested in resolution. We are aware of many long-term conflicts which can have almost immediate resolutions. This is because there is a truth which exists contrary to postures.

We would suggest this service be taken advantage of for any conflict for which you would like resolution. You may contact us for participation in conflict resolution.

This can be done in complete confidentiality.

Many of the situations in which you see and experience conflict are not approached for resolution, but we suggest that all conflicts can be approached. Often the flaw in the current model of negotiation is that a third-party does not exist, or a third-party does not approach each of the two parties to a conflict.

In our process, any conflict which exists is seen from the perspective of those in conflict. While current conflicts may not have provided us with permissions, scores of similar conflicts have provided us permissions, so there are common issues, though the details are all different. With permission, we can access the emotions, thoughts and facts surrounding an issue from the perspective of each side of the conflict. These are the variables.

We then run all the probabilities given the variables. We understand that on earth you do not have the ability to simulate projections of probably realities. However, it is possible for you to receive the results from such simulations. These simulations normally contain the resolution. From the relative strength of the probable outcomes, we can discern the best solution. The best solution is the one which each side will find acceptable enough to maintain over the course of time.

In closing, we simply offer that we are available to assist in ending conflict without public acknowledgement or awareness, and do so simply as a public service.

A Stable Economy

In this section, we seek to present a stable economy and how this can be achieved. A stable economy means an economic situation for you where you know your economic status and that status is good by your standards if you are being honest. If your status is not good, then the design for stability is itself based on some dishonesty and therefore is not stable. It may take years, decades or even a century or two, but it will fail. It is some form of economy you are subject to but over which you have no control..

The earth can have a stable economy. The off-world concept of this includes wealth and security for all. The lack of economic equalization creates great disparity on earth. For example, everyone who survives has a place to sleep and put their things, and enough food so they do not starve. If you are in a third world country, this might be $500 a year. If you live in Manhattan or San Francisco, this might be $200,000 a year. Certainly, the quality of life is dramatically different. But the basic components of living are the same: food, clothing, and shelter.

There are several historical precedents which remain in the belief system of humans. First, there is a scarcity mentality. While this may be true if you want authentic Gucci wardrobe, this is not true if you are satisfied with something that looks like Gucci but may be more durable and is reasonable in cost.

There is enough land and raw materials to build a home for everyone. Humans have figured out how to grow enough food for their populations in the first world.

The third world works on different goals. In the third world, with a high birth rate, there will never be enough resources. The problem is the birth rate and overpopulation and there is a reason for this.

So, in this model for understanding the mentality of scarcity, the third world is still subject to scarcity, but the first world has overcome this. This does not suggest that there are no people going hungry in the first world, it is to suggest that the first world knows how to grow enough food for its population. That there is enough land to live upon, enough raw materials to build homes, and an ability to grow enough food means there is not a scarcity. Scarcity is not the problem.

We must make a stable economy as simple as possible because people have beliefs to the contrary, and these will result in many different statements. Because these statements are based on their beliefs and experience, we must change their experience before their belief can change. In the interim, they still believe in an unstable economy, but are living in a more stable economy.

This contradiction between belief and reality generates specific behaviors. We hope to address the main behaviors and the variety of economic mechanisms employed by humans to achieve stability in an unstable economy. The progression then is to eliminate scarcity and document the mechanisms used by people to achieve stability.

If a description and understanding of the mechanisms is available, the best case is that those who employ those mechanisms will recognize that scarcity has been eliminated and therefore the need to achieve stability at any consequence to others is no longer necessary.

Our estimate is that there is a good chance 10% of people can adapt relatively quickly, quickly enough to stop extinction. The 90% of humans will not adapt quickly or not at all. In this model, the 90% may not survive, which means decimation. Decimation may not mean extinction for everyone, but may be extinction for you.

On the other hand, it could be that 25% or even 50% adapt relatively quickly. The difference between a large number adapting quickly will be access to truth. How long does the pantry have to be full for you to stop fearing you will starve? For some, there will never be a change in this fear. Think of someone who never had enough to eat as a child. For some, it may happen within a matter of a year or two. Some do not have this fear.

Access to truth enables us to understand why we feel the way we do. Understanding the basis of our feelings, which may be hard for us to figure out, is the beginning of changing our beliefs. This is the reconciliation of events which happened in the past, and that changes have been made so those events will not happen again. This situation does not mean that individuals will deal with their fears. To overcome fear normally requires intention to overcome fear.

We have provided a description of having land, a home and food for about 20% of what it now costs you with Simple Land, Simple Home, and Simple Farming.

In practice, if you think of doubling or tripling your income, you would consider yourself to be much more wealthy and secure than you do right now. So, while there are many details we didn't discuss here, what is important is the concept. If you can understand the concept, the details can be determined which do not undermine the concept: you will have much more wealth with Simple Land, Simple Home, and Simple Farming.

While some will keep the extra money they obtain and become truly wealthy and secure, most will not. The reason for this is their system of belief. We will go over the most common of these belief systems to provide a way for those who want to stop extinction to do so instead of perpetuating their belief systems.

We anticipate at least 10% will want to stop extinction, and perhaps up to 50%. The rest are unable to be concerned with their beliefs nor extinction. This is cause for sadness and may cause the death of their families and large groups of people. We should not expect that they can overcome errors in their beliefs when they cannot. If you can understand there is potentially a process to stopping extinction which can be pursued, then you have done well.

So, now, we will provide a description of the belief systems and fears which generate obstacles to stopping extinction. Most of the people with these beliefs systems and fears would say they do not want extinction to occur. But, as far as taking any action for this goal, they just don't feel it's necessary or do not know what to do.

In third world countries, focus is currently on survival because it is required. So, to assist those countries in stopping extinction through providing a better quality of life, we first have to make stopping extinction possible in America.

It is easier in America because large numbers of Americans believe in a comfortable lifestyle. The tasks in America are then to provide the opportunity for this lifestyle to all citizens. This is the purpose of Simple Land, Simple Home, and Simple Farming.

So, there are two contrary systems which maintain the requirement for the focus upon survival in America. These are speculation and Advantagist behavior.

Advantagist

As explained in other sections, Advantagist is our name for the behavior which is utilizes the instinct to survive but applies this instinct not to animal predators and a lack of food sources, but to other humans in a developed civilization. To be clear, an Advantagist is someone who goes to college and makes more money than double the minimum wage in their career.

So, if you went to college or just applied yourself to achieve similar skills and have been able to achieve a significantly higher wage, you are what we call an Advantagist. The Advantage is the higher wage which on the scale of hundreds of millions of people creates an economic underclass.

This result is characterized as a choice to be successful or not, rather than an accurate description that between fifty and seventy-five percent of any group of people will not achieve Advantagist status. This is due to universal design factors which are not acknowledged nor consciously known by those who promote the Advantagist model.

While the definition of these factors is available Off-World, on earth a characterization which can be accepted might be that a person "is good with their hands" and not inclined to study higher mathematics. Other characterizations might be that someone is supportive of others or willing to walk into a burning building. Altogether, this group is more than half of humanity.

The truth is that these factors exist and ignoring these factors has resulted in an economic underclass. This ignores the basis of our common understanding which is that all men are created equal. In the terms of our presentation, this does not support human rights, specifically the Right to Equality.

This situation was not malicious in creation. With the development of modern civilization by America after World War II, higher education increased exponentially and the jobs which needed this education increased and offered better pay, so this was a way to achieve a better life. This is not a flaw in the development of our society, it was natural coming from the Great Depression and prior eras where survival was not assured.

We don't need to continue what has happened in the past or dwell on it. We need to develop to the next stage and make is possible for everyone to achieve the wealth and security that successful Advantagists enjoy.

We Americans are the living embodiment of the maturation of a civilization and a planet. However, most of those planets go extinct, so we must take the appropriate steps so that we are in the group which survives. Currently, we are not in the group that survives, we are in the group which goes extinct.

We need to learn to understand that there is a model for this and that there is a larger galactic community Off-World. We can overtly participate in that community which enables wealth and security for all. Anyone would naturally ask, "Where is the proof?"

The Off-World community is happy to offer proof on your terms. Proof on your terms means proof to everyone on the terms they specify, because proof to someone else is not proof to you.

It is understood by those with access to the human design that humans are not designed to accept proof given to another automatically. Some may relinquish that reservation, but it is not inherent in human design.

In some groups in America, Advantagist are called Elites, and these groups may characterize themselves as "left behind". This characterization of Elites and left behind are generally accurate. We do not employ those terms because our concepts are specific to our perspective, and we do not formally represent the groups of people who employ those terms. That said, their assessment contains the truth. Correction of this situation and ending this conflict is important, and our solutions will do this.

The Advantagist is considered ambitious to varying extents but is generally willing to work hard and get educated to obtain a better income and the lifestyle accorded that level of income. This is considered admirable, and it is. So, on a personal basis, this is a good idea to improve your quality of life. On the level of a civilization, this means that the Advantagist group creates an underclass of citizens who do not do this.

The main error in this design is the dishonesty that everyone can be an Advantagist. While it may be true that this is technically possible, it does not recognize the structure of human design which is based on designs employed throughout this galaxy and universe.

Specifically, most people are not concerned or oriented to higher education nor have the ambitions to get ahead of others. Their focus is different, and no less important or acceptable than any focus which supports human rights. The people who have been left behind are made to feel they are less than or despicable in some way. This attitude is dishonest and inaccurate, and is not sustainable.

While it may seem that encouraging everyone to go to college is a good idea, historically college has been for people who have a proclivity for the study of knowledge, which is, universally, about 14% of the population, with an additional similar percentage of the remainder of the population.

There are a couple reasons for this encouragement. The first is that this encouragement provides a rationale for Advantagist behavior and adherence to a Right to Equality. To be clear, Advantagist behavior does not support human rights, specifically the Right to Equality. In simple terms, there are Elites and they have created an excuse for leaving you behind. So, Advantagists project that being an Advantagist is available to everyone, and it is the choice or laziness of an individual who does not pursue being an Advantagist. This makes it the fault of an individual that they are part of an economic underclass or poor, and not the fault of the Advantagist.

Cartels

Advantagist behavior results in cartels. In our description, a cartel is a group of people of a profession or industry where that group has achieved financial advantage. For example, a person may have a forty year career. If they attend college for four years, they give up 10% of their income years. This would suggest they would deserve a bit more than 10% more income to compensate for their investment. However, in most cartels, their income is double. In some cartels, their income is tripled and quadrupled. This has created the economic underclass. Perhaps, more accurately, it has perpetuated and increased the size of an economic underclass which originally was the immigrants from Europe in the nineteenth century.

Basically, this is a system which provides great financial benefit to some. It would be the Advantagist position that they are just trying to make something of themselves and attain greater wealth than they would otherwise have. What has happened in the past cannot be changed and is not the focus of this presentation. Our focus is to provide a better life for those who are not Advantagists or Elites.

For most people to participate in the Advantagist model, a higher education or special ability is required. With the development of advanced technologies, a criterion for ability has emerged which cannot necessarily be provided by higher education.

For example, a software programmer often learns this skill on their own, and often those who attempt to learn this skill in college do not excel. This is because education and experience are not intelligence. From our perspective, intelligence gives you the ability to analyze and envision probabilities.

In history prior to this century, higher education was for very smart people and upper classes. Highly educated people did not have 10 times the advantage over others, but their advantage was largely dependent on class. So, poor doctors, lawyers and professors was a reality.

But now, getting a higher education is a successful way to obtain a better life compared to other people, meaning you get a much greater income. While one cartel, education, would assert than anyone can do this, that assertion is dishonest.

So, for example, a more honest perspective is used in some parts of Europe, which is during high school, the decision is made if you are going to higher education or not. If not, you are trained for a trade and may enter apprenticeship. This is a model which is based on truth.

This truth is challenging for the educational cartel because of their dishonesty. Their assertion of their right to have a better life than others is that anyone can go to college and get what they got. This may be technically possible but is not accurate.

In some areas, 85% of the students who educators convince to go to college stop going to college. They stop college once that influence is not pressuring them and they see what college is actually about.

College is about books, studying, thinking, and communicating those thoughts in written and verbal methods. In the Advantagist system, this is typically done with the goal of attaining an advantage over others in one of professions which make up the cartels.

Some people like books, others do not. Some people like to read fiction, but don't like studying. If you do not like books, then it is not good work to have you focus on something you do not like. You would find that people who do not like books too much do find some type of work acceptable or even enjoyable.

Off-world, we observe that 14% of people are focused on knowledge, while 86% of the population are not focused on knowledge. Of that 86%, half do enjoy books but education not so much, the other half do not like books nor education. Those who like books usually find reading fiction to be entertaining. We provide overview here for basic groups of people, and specifics will provide greater insight.

Speculation

The next activity which is contrary to a stable economy is speculation. Here, we differentiate between speculation and innovation. Speculation is economic gambling on something which exists. Innovation here is the creation of something. It may be that something which exists undergoes an innovation, however, as something exists already, such innovation simply increases the value of that which exists.

Speculation in the American economy is largely based in two industries: real estate and stock markets. These are the cause of instability in the American economy. Rather than a mechanism for improving the quality of life, they are a mechanism for accretion which we are using to mean financial concentration. Basically, these are the methods which result in 1% of the population having more than 50% of the wealth.

Typically, in human history, such a concentration is cause for revolution. Unfortunately, while a revolution removes the current leadership, it does not change the culture, and so the new leadership usually has the same understanding of culture as the leadership it replaces.

With real estate, the understanding is that inflation is caused by the increase in the cost of homes. The financial mechanism by which the wealth is transferred to 1% of the population is clever. If you sell a property for more than you paid, you gain the difference as profit. So, this enables the real estate speculator to gain wealth and a better quality of life.

Because this process is ongoing, people who buy a home and sell it several years later see a profit. However, most of most mortgage payments is interest. So, you aren't paying for real estate, you are paying interest. This is illusion. You paid the interest all those years and you get the money back when you sell. But the next buyer pays interest on the inflated value they paid. This is a model based on inflation. Such models can only inflate so far before they collapse and repeat. This could be seen as re-assessment of the value of locations, which is the basis of the cycle. The important part is that the interest paid in the cycle is the amount taken from the economy which everyone pays for as inflation.

If you were to pay a mortgage beyond half the term, you pay more towards the real estate and less in interest. However, most people move from one property to another, riding inflation, and so interest remains the majority of their payments.

Basically, the correction for this speculation is Simple Land and Simple Home.

The Simple Land model provides a citizen with the right to have and use a plot of land to every American to live upon for the duration of their lives. The example uses 1/8 of an acre as the size, but this can be any size which can be set by the citizens.

The Simple Homes model suggests that a modest home, perhaps 1000-1500 square feet can be authorized. These homes be financed for a hundred year mortgage because a decently maintained home is viable for at least 100 years.

Interest could be zero percent or 1% or 2%. In this model, the country is financing homes for its citizens, or it could be currently analyzed that citizens are setting up a national financing for individual homes.

It could be a county could develop a program for municipal bonds which accomplishes this. For example, the county tax received from new residents and business would pay for the yield required to incentivize municipal bonds. The businesses get happy people to work for them, the people get mortgages which cost almost nothing, and the county grows and prospers.

For example, with zero percent interest, if the funds were obtained through bond, the government would have to pay the interest. The amount of interest would be dependent on the incentive needed to sell the bonds. As the dollar currency is not tied to a hard standard, such as gold, there are valid questions of how much currency is in circulation and how much is held by people as a security, and how the value is changed printing more.

While there may be precise answers to these questions, they are not in the public domain. Put simply, we as American citizens can provide ourselves with wealth by providing very low interest loans for home construction. For example, a $100,000 loan for a 100 year mortgage is $1000 a year, which is a monthly mortgage of $83. $100,000 is currently adequate for a manufactured home greater than 1000 square feet in size. If Simple Land provides you with land to live upon, then your home cost is $83 a month.

Contrary to what you have grown accustomed to, this cost is very similar to the relative cost of a home before World War II. This is not a new concept; this is a birthright we seek to obtain again as it has been taken. The mechanisms for the extraction of our wealth and its delivery to 1% of the population is clever and complex, but we can have a simple solution and repair. We are the citizens of this country, and can easily stop our enslavement to mortgages.

Existing housing prices are significantly more than these amounts in most states, so this will provide a method of keeping existing home prices in check. For example, it may currently cost $3000 a month for a mortgage in an existing city. An $83 mortgage means that you can accumulate nearly $3000 a month with Simple Land and Home. So, that housing price will drop because you can only sell a home for what someone will pay. The existing

157

home is probably a more desirable location, but how much more desirable? The market will determine this.

Advantagists who benefit from the current economy will find fault using contrived issues. The basic concept is that we as American citizens have a right to a plot of land in this country to live upon. Our main economic goal as citizens should be to provide ourselves with a home on that land with a mortgage at the lowest interest possible interest rate for a duration which reflects the usable lifetime of the home.

Citizens own the country; citizens can make these determinations. While wholesale application of this model in a year would cause significant economic consequence, a rollout of 5% a year would take 20 years. I would anticipate that 1% a year is very ambitious, and that would be wise, because a transition to a different basis will take place over time.

So, in the most populous state of California, there may be 7 million homes, and so 1% would be 70,000 Simple Land and Homes. So, at 1/8th of an acre, this would be 10,000 acres or 17 square miles. 70,000 mortgages at $100,000 would be $7 billion in mortgages, which is not that uncommon for a bond amount. 1% interest on $7 billion would be $70 million. So, if the state offered a bond with 1% and paid the 1%, those 70,000 homes would have a 0% interest mortgage of $83. Now.

In lower population states, this can be done without much consequence right now.

Rather than thinking this would hurt the economy, this will expand the economy exponentially. While your money is certainly enjoyed by the 1% who get all the benefit from you working your life away, if you keep the money instead, you can have a better quality of life. This means spending a portion of the money you keep, which increases the economy, i.e., you are spending money. The portion you save makes you wealthy.

Stock Market

Stock markets are the other speculative instrument. This can be corrected and brought into reality as well.

Basically, the stock market is a sort of lotto where valuation is not based on value. While it would appear you might win this lotto, this is not the case. There are winners, but if you have a job, you are not one of those people.

Currently, the value of a stock is what someone will pay for it. So, stock market prices rise and fall based on confidence in the company. This works incredibly well for stockbrokers, not so much if you are their clients. Again, just assume you get 10% of the profit and they get 90% of the profit. This is the purpose of their job. How this is done is complex and there are legal methods for these manipulations. You are looking at 7-10% appreciation in the value of your portfolio and so you think you are doing great. 50% of the wealth still lands with 1% of the population.

To correct the stock market is easy, but this takes away your chance at the lotto, and more than that, takes away 1% keeping almost all your potential profits. But they were never your profits because the system is far more complex than that. The explanation is clear off-world but would only cause incredible denials by the perpetrators. The good news is that this can easily be corrected to your benefit.

To do this, we change from speculative value to investment value, which is ROI, or return on investment.

This is currently seen as dividend based stocks, and utility stocks may work on this model, for example.

For many stocks which are speculative instruments, there is normally no dividend. The idea is that if they manage their brand and sales properly, the value of the stock will go up and this is how investors make money. The opposite can happen as well.

An ROI model works on return on your investment. A simple example is that you buy $100 in stock. If the annual dividends are $1, you made 1%. If $5, you made 5%. Some stocks are more reliable than others, so to get a better return, you buy a riskier stock. The market can determine value and risk.

But if you get $7 dividend on $100 of stock, you made 7%. This would diminish the value of the stock if the risk analysis determined that other stocks of that risk profile are yielding more than 7%. Your $100 stock might then only be worth around $60. If the dividend is only $4 next year, you might sell the stock and obtain a different stock which is yielding 7%.

So, in this model, stability in yield through dividends is the basis for stock prices, not speculation. A company would offer a dividend they were sure they could deliver every quarter. This would set the value of the stock. If the company has long term stability, the dividend could be less because it is less likely that the stock price will fall. If the company is new or in a volatile industry, then the yield should be higher, but there is more risk the stock valuation could change.

So, the most stable companies might offer only 2% dividends, but the most volatile companies might offer 7% or more in dividends. The market will determine value based on yield, based on return on investment.

To reinforce this non-speculative model, dividends should not be taxed, and speculation profit should be taxed. Speculation should be taxed because this causes instability in the economy which hurts average citizens. Unless a company is selling shares, they make no money from the speculation of stock owners. It is natural that stockholders want a great quarterly report so the value of their stock increases. Company stock prices can rise and fall over 50% in a year due to perception, when it is still the same company with the same assets, steady sales, and the same market share.

If a company shows dramatic increase in profits and dividends, then for example the company might have an annualized dividend of 10% which could lead to an increase in the valuation of the company. With an increased new valuation, the same dividend might only be 5% yield next quarter.

There is probably a way to determine the taxation required to discourage speculation, but for example, if you own a stock less than a year, you are taxed at 50% on profit from speculation, less than 2 years, 25%. These percentages are examples to show the importance to changing the perspective from speculative to value based stock prices. If you hold a stock for more than 2 years, it is not speculative by our description. You would also show a loss when you bet on a stock and lost money.

This speculation tax would be a simple sheet: you bought how much at what price and sold at what price in less than 1 or 2 years, the difference is profit or loss. If you sold 100 stocks during a year, there would be a line for each stock. There would be no deductions for business expense or anything else. Your profit after speculation tax is your income.

Innovation, on the other hand, takes place when companies are formed. In this model, you are issued stock when you invest in a startup company or are one of the founders. When the company creates a public offering, you make your money back and could make a lot of money. This should not be taxed. This is innovation, how the economy is grown in dramatic ways.

Many times, when a company issues a public offering, they get a large amount of investment, and it may take time for the company to ramp up and use that investment to increase their profit and yield. So, a new company stock valuation may be temporarily based on sales and dividends may not be issued, but this will change within several quarters.

A simple rationale is that you will have a much less stable economy for most citizens with a large portion of the total assets in a speculative market. A stable economy can mean nearly everyone gets a good level of wealth. A speculative economy has significant inflation and deflation. Each cause significant hardship to people. While there are a small percentage of people with large profits in a speculative market, most citizens lose relative wealth.

Simple Pay

In this section, the goal is to present the basis used by our culture for inequality in pay.

To Stop Extinction

In the Simple Pay model, our current pay structure has a ratio for lowest pay to highest pay of infinity but is at least 100,000:1. In other words, the lowest pay in America might be $7 an hour, but the highest pay has no limit, and is more than $1 million an hour based on a 2000 hour work year if someone makes $2 billion per yar. This pay ratio would be about 140,000:1.

To correct this, we would look for reduction of the ratio to 7:1. People who have a passionate negativity to this assertion are extremely frightened, so this is the purpose for them for this assertion: they can identify their fear and a derivation which follows delineates the process which takes place to eliminate this fear. There is no purpose to discussion of this from our perspective, as will also be part of the derivation.

The purpose of the 7:1 pay ratio is that it is a starting point.

Parity in this example means that you would receive additional income for the loss of income for years attending college as well as the cost of college.

If a non-college educated person makes $40,000 and a person with a 4-year degree makes $80,000, the ratio is 2.

If a non-college educated person makes $20,000 and a person with a 4-year degree makes $80,000, the ratio is 4.

These ratios must be adjusted for reduction in years of work because of attending college and college cost. These adjustments increase the ratio because the non-college educated person might work 40 years, but the college educated person worked 36 years and spend a year's income on college, leaving 35 years of income. If the person attended an expensive college, the assumption was that doing so would increase their income even more, raising the ratio even more.

We can probably say the ratio is between 2 and 4 even with the loss of work years attending college and the cost of college: you will make 2 to 4 times the money of someone who did not attend college. This is how the underclass was created and this was done intentionally even though implementation was done by individuals.

So, starting with a 7:1 Pay ratio as the maximum is more than current yields for attending college, so this would not reduce the benefit to the large majority of Advantagists and cartel members.

To reduce the maximum pay ratio to 3:1 would basically create 3 levels of pay: working people,

Advantagists at 2:1, and an executive class at 3:1. Obviously, there is income at every dollar amount, so these are just averages.

To reduce the maximum pay ratio to 2:1 would leave working people and Advantagists. Without Simple Systems to cut expenses in half, this would be income reduction. With Simple Systems, Advantagists still receive great benefit, much more than what they currently receive. The difference would be to non-college educated workers who would receive much more than they currently receive.

To provide parity, probably you would need a maximum pay ratio of 1.5:1 which could be increased by 50% for incentives to 2.25:1 for the most successful Advantagist and the lowest paid worker who earns no bonuses.

There are exceptions to the 7:1 pay ratio. Entertainers and athletes are a good example: they may have any number of years at higher than 7:1 pay ratio, but they may only have 1 year of high pay ratio. So, the number of years of higher than 7:1 pay ratio for these people is not based on a 40 year model. Another example is an invention, of which an inventor may only have 1 which generates higher return than the 7:1 pay ratio. Another example are the founders and investors of a startup. All these exceptions and any others not mentioned are not addressed by the pay ratio. As this is just a presentation, it may start a discussion which would have to deal with such issues.

Another type of exception is if you start a company, the company has great success and then sell your stock. You may achieve an extraordinary wealth, but this is separate from your pay rate.

The typical pay rate which is higher than the 7:1 is executive pay, which in this means someone at a level higher than direct supervisor. A direct supervisor means you interact or supervise or manage people who perform a task. As titles are often arbitrary, this definition is provided. An executive could be a city manager, a CEO, other corporate officers, a director, a general manager, or someone with "vice-" or assistant in front of these title, such as vice-president or assistant director.

Investment careers fall into two groups in this model: those who start companies, and those who buy and sell stock or bonds in some way. Those who buy and sell stocks and bonds rely upon a speculative stock market to achieve pay greater than the 7:1 ratio.

This inequality caused by a high pay ratio must be corrected for a stable economy. The reason is that if this is not solved, there will be an underclass who do not enjoy the same quality of life, and the Advantagist mindset will prevail. The Advantagist mindset is that you must get ahead of others. To create a stable economy, the minimum wage can be raised, or the maximum pay can be lowered, or both. While many who benefit from this inequity are solely focused on maintaining their privilege, the truth is available off-world which can assist these people in changing the behavior from opposing human rights to supporting human rights.

We do not suggest governmental controls. Governmental controls are typically not effective because this simply means that an Advantagist just must find a way around the government controls to get paid at a higher pay ratio. So, minimum wage and maximum wage is not the mechanism which will succeed.

The only mechanism we know of which can solve this within a decade is Activation. Activation can take place if a million people want this correction, which is about 0.5% of adults in America. Activation will be assured if 1.5% of adults in America choose to activate. Activation takes place in concert with Off-World access. In simple terms, an adult in America must decide that they want this, and that decision becomes real with an action.

To summarize this, if there were a 1.5:1 pay ratio, with $10 trillion in wages in America, each adult American who is not one of the exceptions mentioned might make between $40,000 and $60,000.

While this does not seem like much, with Simple Land, Simple Home and Simple Farming, your cost for food and shelter might be $5000, which means that 87% to 92% of your income remains after survival costs.

A model for implementation might utilize a programmed inflation of 100% so that post-inflation incomes go from $80,000 to $120,000. In this way, Simple Systems would reduce housing costs while other costs increase. As incomes would increase, the overall result would be a stable economy with increases all around except for housing, and regulated food cost increases.

Because the current pay ratio is perhaps 100,000:1, this has enabled other ratios to enlarge similarly. For example, the cheapest home to the most expensive home might be $50,000 to $50,000,000 which is 1000:1, but this ratio may be only about

100:1 if we look at per square foot values, such as $20 per square foot to $2000 per square foot.

Correction of these ratios would take place over time and be related to actual values and not speculation. There is no doubt that living on the beach is preferably to most people compared to living in the middle of the desert, so location will always be a factor for real estate, but that doesn't mean that values are appropriate in our current economy.

The Reason to Attend College

It is asserted that this inequality is the market force requirement to compel people to make this investment. This assertion is made by people who are compelled to achievement by the increase in pay. People who are not compelled for this reason would not assert this unless there was an emotional reward for making such an assertion, because this would not be their reasoning.

However, that is not true. It is not true because it assumes that:

1.   People have no preferences.

2.   People have no aptitudes.

3.   People are only compelled to achievement by increase in pay.

All these assumptions can be false.

Logical Analysis of the Inequality of Pay

A derivation of the invalidity of inequal pay is:

1.   If truth exists, it provides a basis for pay. Any other concepts for pay must then be based on a theory that truth does not exist, so there is no rationale against inequality; any rationale provided for or against equality of pay is opinion.

2.   If truth exists, opinion is a form of dishonesty. This is because if a belief is inaccurate, the interpretation of the belief into application to a set of conditions which is stated as an opinion therefore has an invalid premise.

3.   If truth exists, then the reason an individual desires to earn more than others exists.

a.   This does not assert a basis for earning more than others, not deny such a basis, this only asserts that there is a reason an individual desires this.

b.   While this reason could be survival in an environment where existential survival is threatened on an ongoing basis because the instinct to survive is triggered, within a developed civilization such as America, large numbers of people do not starve daily, so this existential threat to survival does not exist due to starvation.

4.   Exposure of truth will show every purpose which results in advantage over others is based on fear.

5.   Truth is the antidote for fear.   The implementation of the antidote to a specific fear is called Implementation herein.

6.   The Implementation has no time standard because the Implementation is by the choice of the individual.

7.   For Implementation to take place, the individual changes their goal from manifestation of advantage over others to Implementation.

8.   The Implementation can take place within 1 lifetime but typically takes up to 100 lifetimes for a given fear. The chances of Implementation taking place are:

a.   .0001% chance in one lifetime, one in 1 million.

b.   The chances of Implementation taking place in 7 lifetimes is 1%.

c.   The chances of Implementation taking place in 100 lifetimes is 50%.

d.   The chances of Implementation taking place in 500 lifetimes is 99.9999%, only 1 in a million Implementations does not take place within 500 lifetimes.

e.   Using this data, an Implementation curve can be created.

f.   Implementation refers to a single fear, not all fears. There are normally many fears. However, Implementation for these fears can be pursued concurrently.

9.   If advantage over others is achieved or pursued, then Implementation is delayed and not pursued.

10.   The truth is that your planning is always for multiple lifetimes. The reason for limited growth is that you do not have access to truth, in this case, your multiple lifetime plan.

11.   The action is not that others try to convince you not to want more than others. The action is by the choice of the individual to solve this problem, which means:

To Stop Extinction

a.   Accessing Truth which exposes the fear and the antidote. If the truth cannot be accessed, the process stops here.

b.   Implementation of the Antidote to Fear.

12.   If inequality in pay is invalid, the only reason to attend college to do a job is because you like the job you can get with college more than the job you can get without college.

Supersession

The Supersession Process

The process to stop extinction is a series of steps. You could handle these steps in a different order than presented here, or handle them simultaneously, so we are looking for progress, not an arbitrary method.

The first three steps are internal to any state or country which wants to stop extinction.

The next steps are for bringing Supersession to other states or countries.

The steps are:

1.   Defining human rights

2.   Ending Conflict

3.   Implementing Simple Systems

4.   End Extinction Causing Actions

The First Step is Human Rights

The first step is for human rights to be defined by a state or country. The 7 Words program does this by including sincerity, honesty, and human rights. Sincerity and honesty are prerequisites because many say they support human rights, but they don't support human rights as we define human rights. Many humans' concept of human rights simply means people shouldn't be killed unless a very big army decides to kill them. To them, living is your human right under some circumstances.

A group of people may decide upon all the 25 human rights in A Definition of Human Rights, or a subset of the human rights.

The human rights of land, home and food ensure survival, so these are pretty much the basis of any chance of success. And, as you will find, many do not believe in this for others. They may believe in these three rights for themselves, just not for others.

The Second Step is Ending Conflict

The second step is ending conflict. Conflict exists because a system does not focus on everyone's issues. Every group or tribe has their own issues, and these issues are part of any successful solution. So, to end conflict you must identify groups of people or tribes, as they exist.

When you consider the issues of people, you could have people who exist in more than one group. For example, you can have political tribes, racial tribes, ethic tribes, religious tribes, etc. This could easily be a dozen tribes.

The Third Step is Simple Systems

The third step is implementation of Simple Systems. With Simple Systems, we provide a method to manifest the human rights. With Simple Systems, we provide a means of conversion from current systems to Simple Systems. It is certainly possible and probable that there are simple systems which are just as simple as the systems we have provided, so these Simple Systems are just an option to show a better way, we would expect any group to modify these systems to their own designs.

The importance of being simple cannot be overstated. If a system is simple, it reduces the system itself being called into question. People in this world spend all their time arguing over stuff, such as where and who should taxes be taken from. This is dishonesty.

A simple tax identifies with the overall funds needed for all government, and then finds a general way to extract the funds which do not focus on one group or another. Then the citizens can decide if they want to adjust spending on any department of the government. The focus and power are with the citizens.

The Fourth Step is Ending Actions Which Cause Extinction

Ending extinction causing actions takes place when people are wealthy and secure. Until they are wealthy and secure, their insecurity is their focus. This is our instinct to survive.

Extinction causing actions are environmental behaviors. While these issues did not cause the possibility of extinction until about a hundred years ago, they are now brought to bear because of overpopulation.

Overpopulation, for a large percentage of humans, is part of the instinct to survive, you can only survive in your old age if you have enough children to care for you. In other areas overpopulation is caused by the lack of human rights, specifically women's rights. The rights which are not given to women start with education and continues with the power to control their lives. So, overpopulation is solved over time by supporting women's rights and providing wealth and security to everyone. As with everything we present, to get to that point involves access to the truth and using truth in this world. We understand that anyone reading this may be mystified by how this would be possible.

We will provide you with proof on your terms, but if you have not figured out how to do these things, it is unlikely you will believe in solutions we present. Let this unfold one step at a time, because while any series of steps may be modified, if we are using the truth as our understanding, solutions are possible.

When we provide you with proof on your terms, your next question will probably be how something is to be done, and we spend hundreds of years with people explaining these things, but we have to provide proof to the next person, so we can give you proof but are limited in time, so we can't answer your next thousand questions all at once.

We are focused on the outcome, so we may have to bend with the needs of any specific group. But generally, our four-step process can work on a state in the USA and possibly can work on the USA. In either case, if a state in the USA achieves the first three steps, the next step is try an apply this to another state or country, or both.

While a state may question how it will get funds to do such a program, funding will become very easy when a state achieves the first three steps. You are not understanding that there are great forces waiting for this to happen.

American Supersession

So, being American, I thought since we have the best country and a unique government structure, that the transmission would focus on correction of problems within the current structure of America. This is possible but stopping extinction cannot be dependent on people who are not concerned with being wealthy and secure and then stopping extinction.

If people are only focused on their own anger and frustration, and revenge they want to apply to others, they are not focused on human rights, ending conflict and simple systems, even though they would benefit greatly. If you want to scorch the earth, congratulations, you are doing this. But there is no backup plan in scorching the earth, your survival is not part of the actions of that emotional behavior.

At the same time, the current leaders on all sides are not focused on ending conflict. They may say they are, but they are not. They are not listening to and acting upon the issues of everyone. They have their opinions and may be willing to hear you out, but it does not change their course. Their course is based on what they believe is best for themselves and may believe what they want is best for everyone or at least the group of people with whom they identify.

Therefore, step two is ending conflict. It is obvious off-world that this issue has not been addressed. This does not say that if this issue is addressed that the conflict will end. As is presented in the section of the book on ending conflict, there are situations where a conflict cannot be resolved. These situations are where human rights of a group are not respected.

This can be anything from not supporting everyone's human rights to genocide. But you will find in most circumstances, a conflict can be ended. We offer this service to any group of people who feel they are not being listened to and supported.

You may not currently believe such a statement; you may not have heard such a statement. But now you have heard this, and it is up to you to get involved in ending conflict. It is not expected that you understand how the conflict which involves you can be resolved, or you would have already resolved it.

But we have access to truth, and it is true that the truth can be used to set you free, which in this case means ending a conflict.

Can American internal conflict be ended? No one has tried, though some may say they have taken a step or two with no results. We see that American internal conflict can be resolved without much difficulty if there are some resources and they are applied correctly.

We would estimate the budget for resolving conflict at perhaps $100 million, though we can probably show significant change for about 10% of that, or $10 million. The resolution we would provide would mean that a large majority of people are agreed within a jurisdiction. As with all our assertions, it is understood that we much provide proof on your terms, this would be included in the cost quoted here.

Currently, hundreds of millions are spent on election campaigns so the money would benefit everyone instead of benefitting the one who gets elected.

Politicians would not agree, but if people participate, the politicians will follow. Basically, a politician may want to make things better for a group of people or just improve their own situation, but the prerequisite for that in both cases is that they have power.

If Americans do the first three steps, then the next step is helping other countries to achieve these three steps.

In theory, this could be done by the American government. The American governments projection is for American interests which only support other countries if that support is in the interest of the American government. So, the American government acts as an entity having its own existence and priorities. So, while this government can have great benefit for other countries, by definition, the priorities of the American government come first. To make things even more frustrating, often the interests of the

American government has little to do with the American people.

So, in its current state, the American government is not the entity to help other countries except for defense. It is possible in the future, but it is not currently possible. But America has not done the first three steps yet.

Supersession would be better done by an independent group which co-ordinates these activities, and the American people can order the government to assist.

State Supersession

A state of the USA may become the state which achieves the first three steps. This would exponentially increase the value of the state. So, any state which can achieve the first three steps can then work with other states or countries.

Supersession for Countries

For a country to achieve the first three steps involves a process which has not been applied on earth. It would be like a Marshall plan. However, a Marshall plan was a program forced upon a defeated enemy who surrendered. As well, it was managed by the American government with their priorities.

For third world countries, there are fundamental issues which must be addressed. These include government and rule of law. So, while Supersession for all countries is the goal, these countries will require great incentives.

For first world countries, most have a significant cultural and historical heritage. This means they have their own way of doing things. So, they can achieve the first three steps on their own with access to truth. The American government would not need to be involved.

To Stop Extinction

Providing the truth will enable addressing these issues once a country has achieved the first three steps.

The process to stop extinction is:

1. Support human rights

2. End conflict

3. Implement Simple Systems

4. End extinction causing actions

To stop extinction, humans must stop polluting. Stopping pollution is our main goal as caretakers of the earth. Many people don't care about this, but many do but don't know how to do anything about the big issues.

The main cause of pollution is overpopulation. Stopping overpopulation does not mean doing anything bad to the people who are alive, it means reducing the future population by giving people education and human rights.

While this is very short, these issues are the work for stopping extinction, but to get there we need to give everyone human rights, end conflict and implement simple systems.

Off-World Technology

There are about 50 off-world technologies which we may be able to bring to earth. There are many more, but 50 is a good starting point.

I don't have specific understanding of how these technologies work. I don't have a working knowledge. This is perhaps comparable to your cell phone, you know how to use it, but you couldn't build one this afternoon.

But I know the technologies exist. For many of these technologies I have a basic understanding of how they work, perhaps like how many of you may understand how a gas engine basically works, but that doesn't mean you know the specific design of components and their manufacture. I have used many of these technologies. For a few technologies, I was a technician at one time or another.

Not knowing the specifics and details is my protection. I can't give you any of these technologies. If you want a technology, I may be able to obtain it for you if I can get off-world parties to agree. But as you don't have a formal off-world relationship with the parties involved, there is no way to get anything.

The communication bridge will be the first step to any technology. This will enable us to access truth, but also any other information which can include technology.

I can contact my off-world source for a technology and see if they will give it to us. That gift will come in the form of blueprints I will provide in the form of a book with drawings, formulas, methods, and descriptions. After delivery of the blueprints, I will provide clarity for anything which is unclear, and provide course correction if a misinterpretation takes the project off course.

The time frame is about 6 months.

I may be able to do more than one project at a time, but not too many.

Technologies

To Stop Extinction

Here are some of the available technologies with description as needed:

• Direct communication with the off-world community. This brings truth to earth which will include technology.

• Reverse global warming.

• Contral weather.

• Clean the atmosphere. This more than 1 technology, there is 1 technology for each aspect of cleaning. So, to get rid of the ozone as the south pole is a different technology than to get rid of carbon-dioxide.

• Energy sources. There are several different technologies as there are several energy sources. So, in general terms, your delivered cost of a kilowatt is 10 cents. So, any device worth noting is 100 times more efficient, so deliver 100 kilowatts for 10 cents. For clarity, none of these energy sources use fossil fuels. Solar, wind, or geothermal are obvious options but not the only ones. The best solar technologies use the sun differently or use the energy of the universe which we may know about, but don't know how to use. I suppose you could use fusion, but that's not on my list and not in general use except by stars.

To Stop Extinction

- Better batteries.

- Technology to clean water on a large scale.

- Provide unlimited fresh water in a specific area.

- Defense for a country or large area.

- Cures and treatments for diseases.

- Fast space travel.

- Go to outer space without using a lot of energy.

- Live off earth without physical deterioration.

- A wide variety of scanning technologies.

- Metals with special benefit.

Technology Project Projections

To be conservative, I would estimate that return will be 10:1 for return to investment over the course of a decade.

Here's a table which generally covers a range of project budgets as I understand them:

To Stop Extinction

Development	Sales	Estimated Return
$10 million	$1 billion	$100 million
$100 million	$10 billion	$1 billion
$1 billion	$100 billion	$10 billion
$10 billion	$1 trillion	$100 billion
$100 billion	$10 trillion	$1 trillion

Planetary Caretaking

In the end, the actual problem is overpopulation by humans.

The solution for overpopulation is active management of all the aspects discussed in this book for all humans.

The solution does not have to be decimation or extinction, but those choices are not up to me.

We are presenting an alternative to decimation or extinction. Our assertion is that over time, we can offer all humans a better life of wealth and success and then humans will want to fix the planet. While this seems a mountain which cannot be climbed, we have provided the tools to do just that.

To get to the point where this is possible, we start with America and then with Supersession offer these benefits to other cultures and countries.

This is not a plan for America, that choice is not ours to make. America could step up and do this, but America would have end dishonesty, end internal conflicts, and change the way it interacts with other countries. Currently, America provides a strong defense for America, which is translated into a defense presence globally, as well as monitoring world activities from the perspective of defending the safety of Americans. Our security forces do a pretty good job, we are still here and safe on a day-to-day basis.

You might assert that this is what the government does without your consent. This is the situation which Simple Government and Simple Vote seek to correct. But within America, there are those who support our international posture and those who oppose it. Probably America cannot be the police for the planet in the way we have been in the past and provide the tools we offer to stop extinction- those are two different roles. We are not suggesting a reduced defense policy for America, this is up to all Americans.

Americans are complicit with tacit approval of this defense strategy. If the solutions offered by the off-world community are used by Americans to gain wealth, security ,and control of their government, then Americans may decide if they want to take on the role of stopping extinction instead of policing the world. As an American, I feel we have done a good job of providing a defensive standard and assistance. We have failed in the situations that we have often chosen our own defense rather than local human rights. The people in those areas and countries feel we do not support freedom because we did not support their freedom. At the end of the day, while this is true, it is also true that any group of people have to support freedom for themselves and be willing to die for it. That is how we got to where we are, our ancestors were willing to die to stop our oppression.

This is the choice we would face. If we select our own defense as our international goal, which assists many countries that do not provide human rights, we have our current situation. Overall, we have helped stabilize the world. This stability is the basis by which we can now point out there is an impending extinction. So, respect for our military is the honest and sincere attitude.

This extinction is caused by overpopulation, which is not generally a problem in the first world. The solution to stop extinction is a different approach than America has taken heretofore. America would have to implement Simple Systems or other systems which have the similar result to take the different approach required to stop extinction.

America's approach has not dealt with overpopulation, it has provided international protection for democracies with the understanding that this provides us with security.

Supersession means providing a different type of support to the world to implement wealth and security instead of leaving billions to struggle to survive every day. In their struggle to survive, they are destroying the planet. In the first world use of technology, we are destroying the planet.

The struggle to survive daily must be changed to the struggle for humanity to stop extinction. Supersession applies the concepts in my three books so that Americans can achieve this wealth and security, but then can offer this to the world as well. Will this offering be made by the entire country, a state or states, or a coalition of people? Will it be offered by another country, or group of countries that does not include America? That is a choice. It is up to Americans to make that choice for themselves.

Planetary Caretaking is the assignment of humans on earth. It is up to humans to take on that role, though humans really have not done this up to now. These books provide a method by which this can be choice of Americans or any other group of humans. As we Americans lead the world in so many ways, my hope is that Americans can change using the systems and methods provided by off-world. If Americans can change, they can help all humans have wealth and security. Then we can fix environmental problems caused by primitive technologies and devastation caused by overpopulation with off-world assistance.

Communication Bridge

Humans do not understand communication with the off-world community. So, our first project is construction of a stable communication bridge.

In the Dr. Strange movie, Dr. Strange is protesting he doesn't believe in mumbo-jumbo when the Ancient One knocks his soul out of his body temporarily to give him proof of that which he does not believe.

I can't knock your soul out of your body, that was a movie, but we are here to provide you with proof on your terms. It is human nature to doubt that which has not been proven to us in our personal experience. What would be proof to you personally without global trauma? Who can I bring to you that would convince you of this? What would they say that would convince you? You don't have to tell anyone but take a moment to decide these things in your mind.

The off-world community has access to all information which does not violate the human right to privacy, so figure out the proof you want with that in mind. I'm pretty sure you never thought of such a thing, so give it some thought. You can grant access to your personal records, and this is usually a prerequisite to obtaining the truth.

Scientists attempt communication with radio waves. There is no basis for this communication method except that radio is the only technology they have. The off-world community does not use radio waves. I can provide correction on this issue.

Our timeline is that with funding it will take 6 months to get operational but uses technology we currently do not have on earth, and there always seems to be bumps in the road that slow things down.

When I say that we will use technology that we don't have on earth, to provide a bit of clarity, our engineers and scientists won't even believe what we are presenting is technology and beyond that it doesn't exist. So, we have no need to present concepts and details for their discussion at this time.

We estimate that this first comm bridge will cost about $10 million, which may seem a lot, but we can get trillions in information and priceless benefit to human quality of life. The most important deliverable is truth: proof on your terms.

Launch

Our Launch has five steps:

1.   Communication Bridge

2.   7 Words

3.   Defining Human Rights

4.   Activation

5.   Simple Land and Home

For the launch to take place, my contacts off-world say that the concepts must become part of the mass consciousness. This is the journey to that point.

A Communication Bridge is the first step, though we don't know when this will be provided. A comm bridge is a stable means of communication with the Off-World. This will provide proof on your terms. To prepare for this, you decide what is proof on your terms.

The comm bridge will also enable receiving the truth on any subject which does not violate your personal privacy. Because we can get the truth on any subject, this will enable us to solve all the problems and have all the tech which we only see in movies.

The requirement could be something like the rest of the steps presented here may be prerequisite. But that is not up to me, I am a liaison to the Off-World. I will present requests; the response comes from the other side.

7 Words is second because it is the intention to be sincere, honest and support human rights. Many feel that they already do this. For them, this step is just an affirmation of what they already believe or just a more precise definition. But it is an important affirmation because it creates a specific energy which connects you to off-world. If you have not thought about 7 Words, then think about it. If it sounds good to you, then realize that. That's it, not hard.

Defining Human rights is the third step. Human rights is often the basis of public and personal protest, but is generic. The correction for this is to provide detail. Human rights must be defined. You must define which human rights you support, which human rights are you talking about when you assert you have rights. To assist in this, the Off-World has provided a list of 25 rights based on what is common throughout the galaxy for species that don't go extinct.

Activation is the fourth step. Activation is the process whereby you will take some simple action at the right time. Typically, this action will take place when you are at home, but you could be anywhere. Typically, this action might be a phone call where you say some words. To be able to take the correct action at the right time, we have to be able to notify you. So, at this time that would mean you give us a way to contact you for action. The action would normally be at most once a month and will normally take you less than ten minutes, hopefully less than five minutes.

We need a million people for activation to work. Maybe a smaller group will work to get things going. Maybe it will take a few million. We will have to try and see.

To do this, you give us a way to contact you. We will not try to sell you anything or send you texts or post stuff all the time. We will contact you in the way you choose with some advance notice about an action you can take at a specific time. That's it.

It is your choice to take the action, and we will not even follow up.

If you want to connect with other people on these issues and share or participate, I'm sure there will be ways. Activation is simply a method by where you as a person can make change happen easily.

Step Five Simple Land and Simple Home. This provides you with wealth and security. This can be done if we have enough people activated. Most people may not believe this is possible, but we don't need the 280 million people in America to believe it, we just need enough.

We can provide the next steps, but these first five steps will change the perspective in America. The current perspective of people is that you can't change or fix the system, and I must take care of myself and my family to survive.

The new perspective is that if we work together in a specific way on specific issues, we can change the system and the world. We can stop extinction.

This will start a better model of change by human agreement.

I might say something is important, but all of you may want something else first. Step five is Simple Land and home, it may be that some other Simple

System has an easier path to implementation, and so you vote to do that first. Or one part of the country can get one Simple System and another part of the country can implement another Simple System. It may be that a Simple System does not have the best design, and so it needs revision. All these scenarios are part of what may happen. I have received and presented concepts to provide wealth and security to you, so you have the time and good reason to stop extinction.

My transmissions don't ever seem to be close to 100% correct. The message from the other side to me is that I got most of the truth.

Your collective vote shows the way. If what you personally want most doesn't happen first, maybe it will happen second. But if a human right is not supported, the work is not done.

I hope we can get insight from off-world on these issues, that is why the comm bridge can help so much. Then we can get insight on how to make something happen without a lot of conflict. I'm not here to tell you what to do, I'm the liaison between you and the off-world community. I have presented human rights, simple systems to achieve those rights, and definition and a concept of solution for problems between humans. If you do these things, you will be wealthy and secure and stop extinction.

Then, our work is done. But that's a long way off, and far from likely, so it's up to you to do what you are able and willing to do. The only way it happens is if you do something instead of nothing.

Foundation

In each Off-World book, the same Foundation is included as part of the appendix which is called Setting the Table.

The Foundation contains foundational information which we feel is needed to understand an Off-World book.

The List of Human Rights

Each human right on the list is explained in the book A Definition of Human Rights:

1.   A human being has the right to safety

2.   A human being has the right to protection

3.   A human being has the right to eat

4.   A human being has the right to land

5.   A human being has the right to home

6.   A human being has the right to education

7.   A human being has the right to own

8.   A human being has the right to work

9.   A human being has the right to commerce

10.   A human being has the right to travel

11.   A human being has the right to family

12.   A human being has the right to tribe

13.   A human being has the right to retire

14.   A human being has the right to care

15.   A human being has the right to equality

16.   A human being has the right of dominion

17.   A human being has the right to privacy

18.   A human being has the right to truth

19.   A human being has the right to think

20.   A human being has the right to expression

21.   A human being has the right to preference

22.   A human being has the right to understand

23.   A human being has children's rights when they are a child.

24.   A human being has parent's rights when they are a parent of a child.

25.   A human being has legal rights

The Off-World Community

There are 8 billion or so people living on earth. If you are not one of these, you are off-world, world meaning earth. Anyone who is not a breathing human is part of what I am calling the off-world community.

There is an illusion of separation between humans on earth and the off-world community. This illusion of separation only applies to humans, and not to the off-world community.

While people don't generally associate beings from other planets and people whose life has ended, entities or archangels, and Christ, this is because they don't understand the nature of the off-world community.

I do. Though my access is primitive and limited while I'm breathing, I can make it work.

For example, when I am off-world and meet someone I know whose life has ended, it is common for them to be perplexed and ask me,

"How is it you can be here (in heaven), you're not supposed to be able to do this. How is it you can see me and talk to me?"

If humans understood the nature of physical reality and the nature of time, then it would be understood that the off-world community is right here with you, your senses do not detect the off-world community. This is by design. I understand the framework, which is the structure of this construction.

Summary

There are 8 billion humans living and breathing in the earthly community.

Everyone else is part of the off-world community.

We are part of the off-world community and offer contact.

We offer to save humans from extinction.

Our chosen method is significant improvement in the quality of human lives.

We offer to repair earth.

Our chosen method is to save earth from humanity without harm to humans.

To Stop Extinction

We are using this method of working with a liaison to avoid global trauma and chaos.

The Design of This Universe

While these names God and Christ are not used much off-world, it is important to Christian Americans to acknowledge God as the one who created the universe and all the souls in it. And this is true. Off-world, a different description of God is used.

In the off-world community, these names and descriptions are part of accurate and comprehensive symbols. Here on earth, they are names in a language. As a human on earth, I understand the off-world descriptions may be too ambiguous to be useful to some humans.

God

The first name is God. We can use the name God for the totality of the universe. It should be obvious that the universe was created, for nothing has ever created itself. It would be honest to say you didn't know who created the universe if you don't, but to assert that no one created the universe exposes an emotional motivation. There is no evidence that anything created itself, let alone the universe. Without additional definition of God, we can simply say God is a name for the creator of the universe.

In the off-world community, God is named more like a concept meaning All That Exists or All There Is, which is a concept of unity. In other words, off-world we know the universe is living and conscious, even though it is not focused into a personality such as humans have when alive on earth.

If you have consciousness and awareness that you are part of a whole, and cannot be separated, then you understand a cohesiveness. If your hand told you that it was separate from you, you wouldn't take it seriously, it's part of you.

The reason God as a term is not used so much off-world is because God connotes a human personality, typically a father figure. While this is not technically accurate, it's a symbol like any other. Obviously, a human person couldn't contain the entire universe, but some personify God as a human, and all humans have a right to believe as they choose.

The basic mistranslation or error in translation which was communicated a few thousand years ago was that man was created in God's image. The intended meaning was lost. The intended meaning was that man was created in an image of Gods. This means an image God had or God imagined man.

In linguistics, translation of possessive pronouns and prepositional phrases is painfully difficult, no more than here.

I'm not sure of the delineation in design, but it is generally understood that God and Christ are the designer of humans. We reference the designer of humans as the designer. Off-world there are archangels or entities who were part of the project. When this life is over for you, you will be able to access the archives on these records, and for validation you will be able to interview these beings on the project to acquires resolution for any aspects you do not understand.

Christ

The second significant name is Christ. Off-world, the symbol for the designer of humans means something like the word messiah. The messiah has his own realm of which we and all in this world are part of. Basically, this is the lower half of the universe, starting with the physical and moving through what some call the realms of heaven. We have tried to provide a good and easy metaphor later in this Foundation in the section A Way to See the World.

Now, in colloquial terms, you can call this consciousness Christ, the son of God. It's not precisely accurate, but it creates a human description, one that we can understand. It's ok, I think. Now, the word Christ originally meant something like vessel or container, it's been a couple thousand years since I spoke Ancient Greek well, so I've given up trying to remember. So, Jesus was a man who became the vessel or Christ for the son of God. Over time, we have come to simply call the son of God Christ. So, this is workable, even though it is a small fragment of the true story. We could provide Christians with significant details of that story, but our observation is that when you are stubborn, you are not looking for information, you are avoiding information. So, in these transmissions, we will refer to the consciousness of the messiah plane, which contains heaven and earth, sometimes as Christ, but more often as the designer.

On earth, naming is important to many. While off-world, a meaning can be conveyed as easily as a name, and so a meaning is preferred. We will use names for clarity. We understand because many believe these figures exist and some don't believe. This disagreement is used to create a significant illusion of separation between these peoples. Your choice is to participate in this illusion of separation or not.

For clarity, it is true that there is what you call a God and Christ, and that this universe was created. Just because science doesn't understand the mechanics of this construction does not mean it constructed itself. That is silly, nothing constructs itself, anything created is created from a greater place. That the design and construction details and drawings are not available to you is by intention.

The designation of Christ as the son of God utilizes human patriarchy, so is inaccurate, but conveys the concept that the Messiah is under God, a part of God. In these transmissions, the Messiah or Christ is often referred to as the designer: the designer of the world and humans and all living creatures.

Christ Events

As is described in the transmission The 5000-Year Message, the messiah can speak through any human the messiah chooses, the messiah is the medium or etheric field in which human bodies exist, ensouled by a soul. In other words, our world and everything in it is part of Christ, so any action is possible by Christ. These actions are often called miracles. This characterization is due to the lack of understanding of the technology applied to a pre-existing structure.

For ease of communication and avoiding conflict, we can call these events Christ Events. Because Christian texts only reference the period of 1000 B.C. to 0 A.D. in the area called the middle east, there is only documentation of one Christ event, and the documentation includes only a small portion of the event.

As best can be discerned through off-world archival review, Christ Events are of two types.

The first type of Christ Event is when a human species upgrade is actuated. It is common knowledge off-world that this has happened at least a dozen times in the last 7 million years. Some are upgrades, some are tangential variations. A couple examples of these variations known in the western world are a bigger version perhaps double the size of other versions and a long-lived version which lived several times the human lifetime. Each of these variations had their own conceptual purpose. The most recent upgrades, which is comparatively well-documented, is the upgrade from Neanderthal to Homo Sapiens. This took place over 40,000 years ago. The story of the middle eastern part of this event has survived as the story of Adam and Eve in the Old Testament.

It should be noted that there were more than Adam and Eve who received the upgrade in the middle east, so that the species could reproduce. The designer placed a failsafe in the DNA where family members cannot reproduce successfully in one of four such reproductions. So, because of this failsafe, either the new species would be immediately mixed with the prior species for reproduction, or if familial reproduction would immediately result in significant degradation of the new species. The simple solution the designer used was that more than Adam and Eve were upgraded so that the new species could reproduce, though this information is not included in surviving texts.

It should be noted that there were not one set of Adam and Eve, but five sets. These created the five races. The designer's five original races were

Caucasian in the middle east, black in Africa, red in Atlantis, brown or Polynesian in Mu, and Asian in Asia. These races have been mixed in the ensuing millennia, especially recently. Of special importance is that the main basis of conflict in America is this original difference introduced by the designer. One can see that the overcoming of this difference is the test of humans. If this is overcome, we can be embraced by the galaxy. America, in this application, serves as the meeting place of the five races and the battleground for this concept. Will fear or love prevail? This will be a precursor to extinction, or the resolution of the conflict. We are here to promote resolution of the conflict. It should be noted that those who promote the conflict are also promoting extinction. This can be witnessed in their common awareness of an event called the rapture. Proper translation of this concept from the off-world symbol based on the meaning would be extinction, not rapture. The return of souls to heaven, or home, when a life is over or ended is given and always true. This cannot be altered by the concepts and beliefs of humans, this is part of the design; this is how it works.

The first type of event is physical, an improvement to the design of the species. The second type of event is psychological. These events have taken place since the last physical upgrade to homo sapiens. The reason is that prior to this physical upgrade, the human species did not include a critical thinking ability, and as a result did not have more than simple tribal organization. Basically, tribes prior to homo sapiens did not get much larger than 150 humans.

The second type of event is when a concept is presented which is intended to improve the understanding of humans. In the Free Will Model which will be described in one of the next sections, the human design includes free will as part of the design specification. As a counterbalance to free will, which generally results in significant conflict, the designer has initiated this second type of event which seeks to pacify the destructive inclinations of humans operating from fear.

Love and fear can be seen as opposites, hate simply being the state of unable to love. Love can be understood to be a human form of truth. The simplest description of love for humans we have is that love can be seen as manifesting in four actions: respecting, appreciating, giving, and receiving. There are many perspectives off-world, and this is true for love as well, so we present this definition which we see as the simplest. Fear is used by humans as the basis for all acts which are in violation of human rights. Therefore, the most important condition for off-world participation is support of human rights. See the transmission A Definition of Human Rights for a thorough list and explanation of human rights.

This second type of event has taken place four times in the last 5000 years. The compilation of the meaning from these four events is provided in the transmission The 5000-Year Message.

There is always agreement by the souls involved to allow this second type of event, psychological events. There have been approximately 30 such events and agreements, usually with more than one soul participating, usually taking place over a period of more than 50 years.

Jesus

We will speak a bit about Jesus as we knew him because there is so much energy from American Christians who want to know. From our experience in heaven, it is not that people want to know about Jesus. For many, often the most startling and painful knowledge is that Jesus did not want followers and di not offer forgiveness to those who accepted him as their savior. That forgiveness was already inherent in being born and came from the designer. So, Jesus, being sincere and honest, would never act as though a power was his which was not his power. Forgiveness is automatic, restitution must still be made for violations of others' human rights.

Jesus was a man. He was a very interesting man, and I am still challenged to understand Christian's adulation of him. Because he was nothing like his American followers.

Jesus has moved forward to a larger existence, which he earned.

If you want to know what he looked like generally, just go to a mosque or synagogue and pick out a tall, middle eastern fellow of average build with a beard and long hair, about 30 years old, if such a person exists.

Jesus didn't want a church. Jesus never had a church.

Jesus accepted that a religion would be generated from the designer event.

His message came from the designer. The designer selected Jesus because he was the best messenger for the message of the event which was forgiveness. However, the message was forgiveness of others who trespass against you, not forgiveness of you if you accept him as your savior. Your relationship with Jesus and the designer existed before you were born and is not changed by any belief you choose in your human life. You have a much larger relationship with the designer than can take place in any lifetime.

Jesus' message came from the designer. In A Way to See the World, we present that your beliefs, and thoughts and feelings and actions create an energy. The resonance of this energy does not exist solely in our minds, this energy resonates off-world, which means it resonates with the designer.

This was true for Jesus as well. In this way, Jesus resonated with the designer better than any other human at the time in the chosen location. Jesus was therefore the best man to project the designer's fourth message, the message of forgiveness.

There has been a formation of church and members who have decided this means if you accept Jesus you are forgiven. There is truth in this, but mainly it is incorrect, and it is not the designer's message through Jesus.

The message was to forgive others who trespass against you.

We have provided a modern detail of this meaning. This is support of human rights, yours and every one else. Those who trespass against you violate your human rights. When you trespass against others, you violate their human rights.

Support of human rights is the same as not trespassing but provides a clearer and more detailed description of what it means to not trespass. This detailed description is provided in A Definition of Human Rights.

If you don't like someone, or something they have done, your task is to forgive them. That you forgive them is not required for forgiveness, that you accept Jesus Christ as your savior is not required for forgiveness, you are already forgiven for the trespasses you have done and will do in the future.

To repeat this specifically: you are already forgiven as a birthright, you do not need to ask for forgiveness, you do not need to accept Jesus or anyone as your savior for forgiveness. To accept Jesus as your savior may elicit a change in your behavior as is your choice, but the act of acceptance as your savior does not in itself grant you anything, and Jesus did not want you to accept him as your savior.

Constantine made this up in the fourth century to get Christians to bow down to him the way Romans bowed down to him as Caesar.

The part left out is that restitution will be required for the violation of the human rights of others. When the lord says vengeance is mine, this means that you are not the one who extracts vengeance. Violations of the human rights of others incurs debt, or karma, and will require restitution at the time of your choosing.

It is equally difficult to resist vengeance. This the fourth of the designer's messages because it is the most important and the most difficult. If you support human rights, then you do not violate human rights with vengeance.

That you will be forgiven is inherent. You do not have to accept Jesus or Christ to be forgiven. How is it you think you can speak for the designer of humans and decide who is forgiven? The designer already forgave you before you trespassed. How is it you think the designer is bound by time? The designer created our experience of time as moments and experiences it all at once, continuously.

As presented in A Way to See the World, Christ is the world we live in, Christ is the recorder of thoughts and feelings and beliefs and actions. The body you inhabit is Christ's work, you cannot exist at any point where you are not using the world he designed. There is no price for this, it's a gift, do with it as you please. However, the designer is not responsible for your choices. One purpose of being human is to understand that you can choose who you become.

It's hard for us to understand the world this way. It is somehow easier to see Christ as the ocean, and we are the bottles of water in the ocean. The ocean and the bottles and the water are all Christ's design and invention.

Now, some have trauma which is the result of a violation of their rights, and their behavior is a response to that trauma. When that behavior violates the rights of other, they will still incur debt. Now, it would be much better if you did not violate the rights of another, if you can control yourself. No one ever plans to incur debt in a life, the incurring of debt always causes one pain, and the restitution much more pain.

This does not mean you have to enjoy what you do not enjoy. This does not mean you should be happy when you are sad. This does not mean you should love yourself when you cannot. This does not mean you should not scream when you are angry. Though if you scream at others or in their presence, they may not want to associate with you, and that is simply exerting their right to preference.

It does mean that even though it doesn't feel like it, in the ways that matter, you are never alone.

The Logic of the Construction of the Universe

This is a simple 4 step progression of logic we apply, which we call The Logic of Construction of the Universe. While this is a simple symbol off-world, we cannot think of more concise wording. The Logic of the Construction of the Universe is subject to your review:

1.   Nothing creates itself, therefore the universe was created

2.   If the universe was created, there must be a design for the universe which set the rules by which the universe exists

3.   You do not have these design details and drawings, the one who has the design details and drawings has not given them to you.

4.   It must be the intention of the designer that you are not overtly given the design details and drawings.

For clarity, and as a comfort to self-proclaimed atheists, it is true that God is not a guy in a robe with a long beard. It is also true that God and Christ are not humans sitting on clouds to whom you will sit next to for eternity. In this situation, your assertion is correct that God and Christ cannot be human or human-like, especially the two characteristics of being Caucasian males.

For those who understand this, your expectation that others would be able to grow beyond this concept is obviously in error. The error in this case is yours if your expectation of others is based on your understanding or beliefs. In other words, because you have a larger understanding of the universe does not mean others are capable of this larger understanding of truth. The larger understanding is that a human could not have created the universe. You benefit from this awareness; it is worth giving yourself credit for reaching this comprehension.

It is important to understand that we each have a right to belief, and those beliefs define a state we experience. This experience of the manifestation of a life derived from beliefs and thoughts and feelings is the purpose of your life and all human lives.

Your denial of what you know is logical due to your feelings is your right. The next step after this denial is to want to know and to understand. Typically, there is an anger or frustration that is if a larger design is correct, it should somehow be conveyed to you.

The purpose of the Logic of the Construction of the Universe is to offer you understanding without any attached descriptions. A state of denial is just the starting position in the progression you experience. You can refuse to listen and think for as long as you like, and a great portion of humans do just that.

After our lives are over, we will look back and want to know what was true and what was a mistake. This may take a century for those who strongly refuse to think or listen, because everyone has a right to do as they choose. In all these choices, there was an overriding emotion which compelled a person to do what they did, and that is the learning.

We say the next step because you are not alone in this state, it is shared by many, and for most the next step is to want to know. We can assist in this, but you would have to be able to conclude in your own mind that you want to know and change from a state of denial. You cannot and will not be forced to change, the right of free will inherently include the right to be in error, that is the purpose of free will: to enable you and give you the right to be in error and experience the result of that error personally.

Meet and Greet in Heaven

In closing, let me try this. I work with a group, and all of us who do this work can tell stories of people whose body has died, and they won't even listen to their mom or dad or spouse because they know and believe completely that Jesus is going to meet them when they pass over, or Christ, or God, or Moses, or we don't know who, their third-grade teacher. So, anything else is a trick, most commonly a trick of the devil.

Every perspective has a price, and for so many perspectives the price is higher than I am willing to pay any more, i.e., I'm too old for this. I sigh a big sigh before I dive in to help such a poor soul, the price and restitution of my own perspective long ago. How many more payments have I got to go?

"Ok, guys," I say to the team, "who is going to play Jesus this time so this poor soul will listen to the truth." Jesus has moved way past meet and greet at the pearly gates. Don't you think he earned it?

Great, it's my turn. The hard part if figuring out what the poor soul expects Jesus to look like. And then I find out they are not expecting Jesus at all, they believe they are not worthy of Jesus' attention.

And what the poor soul doesn't know is that the truth is much better than what they believe and fear, the truth is infinitely better, unbelievably better. The benefit of the truth to them personally is incredible. But they have a whole bunch of fear, and their fear resulted in a very stubborn inaccurate belief.

If only we can get them to listen. And they sit there, hands over their ears, eyes closed, chanting "I'm not listening, you're the devil, I know who is coming for me any second. I refuse, I refuse, I refuse. Go away." This can go on for years, so we try for longest time and then just come back later, it may take them a week or a century to calm down.

There's no shortage of time, so no big deal. Eventually, one of us figures out how to get the poor soul to listen, he believed that his first pastor when he was a kid would be in heaven to guide him. If we can find the pastor, our work is done. Just another fun time off-world.

Summary

There are two significant names with regards to the design of the universe.

The first is God and the second is Christ.

God created the universe.

Christ designed humans and all other life.

God and Christ are not human, nor like a human.

Christ Events are when Christ uses a human to provide guidance or understanding to humans or when a species upgrade is done.

For example, Christ used Jesus to provide a guidance to humans: forgive others who trespass against you.

A Way to Understand the World

There is a way to see the world, which I hope will add clarity. You may have heard of this metaphor; a few teachers tell variations.

So, there is an ocean. In the ocean there are bottles of water.

Each bottle is a person. It appears to each person that they are separate from all the other bottles, and it appears they are in the ocean but not part of the ocean.

This ocean of water is the field we find ourselves in. By field, I mean an etheric field. All space is like an ocean which is a conscious, aware, listening, observing; an active part of the designer. In this model, the world we live in is an imagining of the designer, with all of us and all our stuff.

The field is not just conscious, the designer created the field and is the field. The designer created the ocean, the water, and the bottles. We arrive as souls in this neighborhood of the galaxy to participate in what the designer offers. And when we first see earth, it is Disneyland times a million, we cannot believe it. We cannot believe our luck because it is free for us to use.

This is not a task of making something and walking away, the field is a part of the designer. The designer is not separate from the physical world, the designer is the physical world, and we are part of this. As a soul, we can choose and have our own thoughts and feelings.

The universe is not an accident of elements interacting; it is by design. That you experience separation in your skin and thoughts is not by accident, it is by design. The world we experience is a field which is the designer.

Think of it, we come into a body, get to control the body, and live a life. And then it is over. But the entire life is recorded in 3 dimensions complete with all your thoughts and feelings.

Time is even better. You experience time as a linear series of events while you are a bottle. But time is part of the field. Time is part of the design. God created all souls at the time of the big bang. The designer created, designed the world we get to experience. Time is part of the design to create experience.

As they created time, they are the masters of time, they are not part of time, time is one of their tools, one of their inventions. They are not marked by time; they use time to mark. Like a series of notches in a piece of wood. Or beats on a drum.

The time does not control the designer, like the notches do not control the one who makes them in the wood. They use the notches to enable you to have experience, they create the seconds and design you to experience each second, one at a time, and have a thought in one second, a hope in another, and an action in another.

We were each created as souls, sparks with a consciousness of our own, so that we could do these things in the field, and the designer beats the drum, and with each beat, we take another step, think another thought, feel another emotion, and then we act.

Our actions are not controlled, our power to choose actions is the purpose of life. We are let loose on the earth. However, each soul who becomes a human has rights. And to ignore these rights means you don't understand the pain your ignorance will cause.

The ramifications of our thoughts, feelings and beliefs and actions are not immediate. But the

237

ramifications are often much more significant that the act. You can kill someone with a thought, a feeling, and an act in a second.

Restitution may take you hundreds of years, even millennia. You will be given all the years you need, take a century, take millennia, but restitution will be made. Someone dies in a second. One second, they are alive, one second, they are dead. But restitution takes all the time in the world.

Will you be forgiven? You were always forgiven. You were never in a state of not being forgiven. Only someone who wanted you to obey them would assert such a threat that you would not be forgiven.

Anyone who asserts that you are not forgiven is dishonest, they are making up stuff way beyond their pay grade, or simply perpetuating dishonesty because it suits them. Perhaps they use fear as a motivation to influence behavior, especially behavior which is beneficial to them. Appreciation is a part of love, they may be looking for love, but you do not generate love by being dishonest. If you have no proof of what we are saying and cannot get proof yourself, you are best not to make such dishonest statements to exert influence over people. I know, you will be forgiven because the end justifies the means. You can tell yourself this for eons, it is never true and never was true.

But it is simpler than that for many, if you are forgiven, you have advantage. Only someone who wanted advantage over others would embrace such an idea. So, yes, you will be forgiven. But you still got to do the restitution. Take your time, whenever you are ready.

Where is the mark of our acts? Where is the recording? The mark is in the ocean where we are in our bottles, in the field we call the world and the universe.

This is why there are 3 guides given: sincerity, honesty, and support of human rights. If you follow these, you will not hurt others. This is the design of the designer. This is a universal concept which has been said in many forms such as the golden rule or the 10 Commandments.

So, in our ocean, our etheric field, every action is not just an action. Each act works like a spark if the act supports the rights of another. Or has no power or energy if it does not support the rights of others.

Because the ocean is a field, an etheric field, and a unified field, that which exists in every drop, everything is any drop is available to us in every drop. So, string theory is correct, but physicists are looking at the wrong fields, quantum entanglement is a small part of this lacking inherent intelligence. Every particle is connected by design. Even though as humans we are cut off from these connections during our lives. Maybe we think we can feel the connections sometimes, and probably we do.

So, we humans face some challenges. Our design overwhelms us, and we cannot focus. This is part of the design. But that does not mean we are doomed. It is known by the designer, designed by the designer, that we would most likely find ourselves in this situation.

So, what solution does the designer offer? A solution is offered, but it is not the designer stepping in and fixing everything.

The solution to this puzzle is obvious, but you must be sincere.

We fill our ocean with sparks or with darkness.

The ocean contains everything we need-everything which exists is part of the design, and everything which is possible. All the tech, all the environmental solutions, all the social solutions, all the economic solutions.

So, why hasn't someone brought them forward before? Solutions are constantly being given, but who will listen?

The things you want may not be here in your living room, but they are connected to you in your living room, even though they may come from light years away, somehow, they are available here and now.

How do we get the solutions which are sitting in your living room? We fill the ocean with sparks or with holes. Sincerity and honesty, we can only do those ourselves. We only got one requirement: supporting the rights of others.

Summary

The designer is like an ocean. In this ocean, there are bottles of water. Humans are the bottles of water. We feel like we are separate from the ocean, but we are part of the ocean.

We experience time as a series of moments, but that is our experience due to our design. The designer does not experience time as we do, the designer is aware of all time and created our experience of time as moments.

You have always been forgiven.

If you violate the human rights of another, there is restitution.

Everything is available to humans. There is no distance between you and all that exists.

Your access to all of this depends on you and all humans.

If you honor the human rights of others, your bottle becomes more transparent, and you increase your participation in the ocean and your access to the ocean.

If you violate the human rights of others, your bottle becomes more opaque, and you decrease you access to the ocean.

Free Will

There is some confusion as to the nature of a free will species. Common Reckoning is something like we have free will or choice. If you belong to a Christian religion, the reckoning may be something like that God gave us free will and will bless us for making good choices.

While this is true, the description is lacking the basis. Off-world, we have access to truth which includes understanding, knowledge, and wisdom. So, there is much less inclination to do things in error, and our ability to do significant damage to anything does not exist.

To design a free will species, understanding, knowledge and wisdom must be blocked. This was done with the design of humans. It sounds difficult, but Christ uses a simple method which works quite well. The mechanism for creating a free will species is that your brain is like an empty hard drive when you are born, you retain no memories or your existence before you were born.

243

While your consciousness has memories, saving to the hard drive is in temp files for the first couple years of your life, your brain doesn't make strong, permanent memories when you are a baby.

As you live in your body for those first couple years, you start to function only from sensory input and learn how to work the body. Think of it, somehow you, a conscious being, can inhabit and operate this body. How does that work? Obviously, you didn't do it, so someone with a lot more skills did it.

Now, mainly because they are frustrated or stubborn or both, some assert consciousness is inherent to biological life. So, this is backwards. Something is always created from a greater place, nothing creates itself. Consciousness is attached to a being though an incredible designer technology which we will cover in the next section Ensoulment.

When this transition has been made to inhabiting and operating the body in 2-3 years, then you start to make permanent memories. This 2-year period is experienced as something like a dream, you are part of the environment, not in control of the environment.

Now, that's a pretty good design for blocking prior knowledge. And it works most of the time. Your soul still has memories, from a different time as a different person using a different language. I have described in another transmission that this type of perception can be called a symbol. How would that symbol be understood in the mind of child in a different place and time speaking a different language? It wouldn't.

Because we don't have prior memories, we make choices based on our inclinations. This is free will.

Living as a human on earth exposes what we truly believe. That's a pretty good design. It is also a very good example of how meaning is lost living on earth.

Free will is certainly a great gift we were given when we were created as souls, which are self-conscious living beings, immortal and indestructible.

We are not separate from all that exists, souls are a unique type of object in this universe, created at the start. We can't have an experience which is separate from God and Christ, they are the universe, the medium in which we exist, even though with our own consciousness it appears we are separate. While we humans want all being to be human, like us, the power which created a billion galaxies is not human, but instead designed humans as a way to experience the earth.

245

To Stop Extinction

Once you have some experience in the universe, we know how to behave. To see what you would do if you forgot all you know, we come to earth to have free will. This means we get to make any mistake we are inclined to make.

Someone told us not to murder, for example, but that doesn't stop people from murdering. So, free will is not a freedom per se, it's more like giving yourself amnesia to see if you truly, deeply learned from your experiences or not.

Summary

Humans are a species with free will.

Humans retain no memories from before they were born.

Humans were designed us this way.

Humans do as we are inclined to do, without remembering what has happened before. This is how free will is enabled.

Ensoulment

When the universe was created with the Big Bang, all souls were created as well. As was given in *The 5000-Year Message*, you are an immortal being, a soul.

A soul has consciousness. Your stream of consciousness, the constant thoughts that go through your head is the stream of consciousness of a soul: you.

At the time of birth, with the first breath, the soul is bound to the body.

For a soul, this is one of the designer's best inventions and technologies.

How does a soul bind to a body, become the inhabitant and the operator? How does a soul own a body, and become the body?

This is incredible. You can imagine the surprise when souls became aware that the designer had created a technology that enables a soul to inhabit a body. Top it off with a new species on a wilderness planet and I was all in. Free? Nice.

The process of binding a soul to a body can be called ensoulment. The process of the soul leaving the body can be called desoulment, but we just call it death.

There is a process. We are going from a place where we are a soul in time and space, to a place where we are a human body.

As humans, we have no memory of this process of the binding of our soul to our body. This is by design. Up till now, there has been no proof for asserting that this process takes place prior to birth. The first breath of life is a good way to view this event. Your soul is attached to the body when the body initially breathes outside the mother.

This is the design of an automated technology we can use but did not make. I compare it to riding a rollercoaster, we can take the ride, but we did not design the ride and do not control the rollercoaster.

You can deny it, you can say you don't believe it, you can fight against the designer's plan, you can scream at God. You saw the empty seat on the rollercoaster and jumped on. You did not have to, you were not forced, you chose to take the ride which is a lifetime.

You can believe with all your being that a body being developed in a womb to be a human is already a human. This is part of the instinct of other mammals who don't have the ability to think critically. But this remains the design of ensoulment.

We use this technology to attach to a body and become a human being when a body is ready for birth. This technology is automated, we can use it, but we didn't design nor invent it. These technologies that the designer designs are beyond a soul's understanding, which means they are very sophisticated. They don't exist like a machine we can go look at and tinker with. For us, they are just how the universe works. At the same time, somebody invented and build this technology and automation, even though there are no buttons, no parts, moving or not, no power plug, and no operator. Ok, somebody knows a lot more than me.

This design protects a human being from being hurt by the acts of man before we are human beings. This design is smarter than we are. You don't have to protect the unborn other than providing a healthy womb, the unborn are not human beings, they are bodies being developed so they can become a human being.

This is not part of your responsibility; you have never been told this is part of your work, and if you were told this, it is not true. The designer of humans is smarter than all humans, his system does not allow acts of humans to destroy the design, the system, and the technology.

Even as a soul in heaven, this is beyond our grasp. Have a little confidence that the design for human beings is generally beyond human tampering.

Mother's Instinct

As with all mammals, it is the mother's strongest instinct to keep that developing body safe. The instinct to keep the developing body safe is often stronger than the instinct to survive. That's how species keep going. If the mom didn't care, the species would end there.

And that mother will think of the body as what it will become: a baby. But it is not a baby till it takes that first breath. Instinctively, moms know this, they wait for the first breath, then her work to have a baby is done. When the baby breathes, sometimes with a spank, the human is born into being.

It is an important common practice now that a baby is held by the mother after birth because it creates that first bond, which moms feel and know instinctively. In our immediate past, it was common that a mother would not get to hold the baby until a bit later. The point we are making is that the question a mother would ask the nurse is, "Is it all right?"

This question is important. It exposes the mother's automatic understanding that while the fetus was developing, preparing to be human, not until the fetus is all right, viable and good on its own, not until then is it a human being.

The body will be owned by a soul and becomes a person when the soul inhabits it with the first breath.

The ensoulment process is not remembered because of the free will design. We don't remember anything before the age of 2 ½. We don't remember being born, and the time prior to birth when we prepared for the big event of our attachment to a physical body. Without any memories, this aspect is just ignored as something without an answer.

Or much worse, people decide that being human starts before birth. Or that a soul is created by a couple people when pregnancy occurs. These ideas are triggered by the instinctive drive. A mother has the instinct to protect a fetus, a developing body.

Until the attachment of the soul at birth, and the body breathes, the body is not viable until that moment. The developing body is not a human being, it is being developed. A body is not a human being, when a soul attaches at birth and breathes, that's a human being.

Even then, the soul can decide it is not ready and back out within a few weeks, and this is called sudden infant death syndrome. It doesn't mean anyone did anything wrong, it's not anyone's fault. The soul realized it was not ready to be a human being and left the body. As part of the ensoulment design, you can exit within a few weeks. The parents of such a baby are often devastated. We can assist with alleviation of this devastation with access to the specific truth from their baby.

Energetic Body

The process which takes place in the background is a soul's attachment to the energetic body. The depiction of the energetic body in the second Thor moive was pretty good. Our eyes can't perceive an energetic body, so until recently there was no such thing. We can't see heat, but it exists, but we can feel it. In the past, if we didn't have a sense to sense something, it didn't exist.

This sensory basis ended with radios and medicine more than a century ago. We accept something exists if we get a tangible benefit at the end, we accept we don't understand and cannot sense how it is done, but if there is a tangible result, it must exist. Science overcame the illusion of control that organic reality provided to humans which was: if I can't detect it with my senses, it doesn't exist.

Those who are trained in detecting the energetic body can do some work with the energetic body. If you couldn't see your physical body, then it would be challenging to describe a human body, and this is true with the energetic body and our five senses.

In the Dr. Strange movies, they constantly work with the energetic body. While that is just a movie and what they do with energetic bodies is inaccurate, it is true that we have an energetic body, and it is like the energetic bodies in the movie.

Just because we haven't given you the technology to view the energetic body yet doesn't mean the technology doesn't exist. But you would have to want the technology, instead of denying the existence of the energetic body and the technology to detect it.

The energetic body is an organization of energy which provides a conduit for the lifeforce. So, this one sentence description has a lot of stuff which doesn't exist for many people, like every word.

An organization of energy is not a concept we have evidence of. Because it is proven and used continuously by us, electricity may be invisible, but we know it is real. When we use the term energy in the phrase organization of energy, we understand the concept of organizing stuff, but we know electricity doesn't work like that. Electricity is electrons which push the next electron which pushes the next electron along wires to a place where it is stored in batteries or used by a device.

When we say organization of energy, what are we talking about? And there's the challenge. Until we completely describe a system, we don't have words to describe it. We haven't made the words up yet. So, with an organization of energy, we immediately go to a place which doesn't exist yet, even though it was in a Thor movie.

If we are talking about electricity as we know it, it isn't organized into forms, it travels on conductive metals when one electron pushes the next electron, and as it does this at the speed of light, we perceive the electricity immediately at the other end of the wire. This is a simple and incomplete description of electricity, which is what we know as energy.

So, is this energy electricity or not? Not. So, first, we are talking about a different type of energy. We use the word energy because it is the only one we have to describe an invisible force which can do things.

So, we can qualify this energy as auric energy, relating to an aura. It is not electricity, which is electrons which behave according to laws of science. But if it is not electrons, what is it? What particles are used? These particles are smaller than electrons and quarks, so they are not going to be detectable with our technology. Which does not mean we cannot provide the means for detection and analysis. We can do this if someone would like this technology.

In the second Thor movie, they have a device with which they can view an energetic body. We don't have this technology yet, but that doesn't mean we can't get it.

This information on the energetic body relates to ensoulment because the energetic body is the system to which our souls can attach. Our soul is connected to the energetic body and the energetic body is connected to the human body.

Think about it for a second, you will leave your body when you die, you are controlling your body right now. How do you control your body right now? Where is the connection between your consciousness and your toes? How does that work? Give yourself the opportunity to understand how this all came about, give yourself the freedom to understand how this all works. All the answers were there, and now a few of those answers are right here for you.

Summary

All souls were created at the time of creation, which can be called the big bang.

You are a soul.

A body is prepared by the mother after she becomes pregnant.

To Stop Extinction

When you are born and take your first breath, your soul attaches to the prepared body.

When you, a soul, attach to a human body at birth, it becomes your body.

This process is one of the designer's technologies and can be called ensoulment. This technology is automated, we did not build it but we can use it.

When you stop breathing, your body dies, and your soul is released from its attachment to your body.

My Part as Liaison

In the movie The Day The Earth Stood Still, the arrival of an alien causes global trauma and chaos. At one point Keanu meets a fellow at McDonald's who has been embedded on earth. I'm like that fellow, the difference is I'm not an alien, not anymore anyway, but I can act as an Off-World Liaison.

What we want to achieve is saving humanity from extinction and saving earth from humanity, without the global trauma and chaos. Humans hurl undauntedly towards extinction and destruction of earth, generally without concern.

Now, 2/3 of species such as humans destroy their planet and themselves. So pending destruction is not a surprise but rather a likelihood. At the same time, 1/3 don't. I am here to help you understand how. Off-world, there is an understanding that humans are in the 2/3 category at the 11th hour.

Humans can be described as an emotionally based, free will species given the right and responsibility for caretaking earth.

Yes, the aliens will come if I call, but I really don't like them. So, because I'm going to need some alien technology for some of these projects, I bit the bullet recently and gave them a call. They showed up within 24 hours, and as I usually do, I ran away, just making sure you guys are still down for the project before I start speaking. I mean, it sounds cool: aliens.

But it's more like dealing with a large lizard or insect or creature, you never know what their game is, but you're pretty sure they don't care about you at all, and it dawns on you they are here for their own reasons, and they have never even heard of my concept of deals and fair play, let alone agreeing to play by my rules. A bit of caution is a good idea.

The good news is that they will give us the tech under the right circumstances, and it doesn't cost us anything. Cost is sort of a human thing, not a universal thing.

I'm sure it seems like fiction, but what I'm going to share is the truth the fictions are based upon. I hope you feel the amazement you felt when you experienced these fictions through reading or in the theater.

Over the last 42,000 years, I have lived about 600 lifetimes on earth. While most finish up in 10,000 years or so, I'm still here. Now that my time here is over, I am one of a few who has been witness to humans moving from first civilizations to this stage, which is either the last stage or a new stage. All I had to do was hang out for forty thousand years.

My interest in earthly life took place after the last upgrade to the species from Neanderthal to Homo Sapiens. These enhancements included some work on the cortex to enable sophisticated mental functions, so it seemed like a good time to jump in.

So, I had the chance to be a part of a new, high-level species on a wilderness planet. What could go wrong?

Perhaps that is a story on its own, but it's not today's story, and for me it was painful enough the first time.

Over the last 10,000 years, about 90 lifetimes, I have developed a special skill set.

There is no title for what I do, so I made up the title Off-World Liaison. I don't know how good of a title it is, but it's the best I could come up with.

Summary

I have access to the Off-World community.

My role is of liaison or facilitator or broker.

My off-world contacts offer technology and solutions to humans.

These are offered without cost but not without condition.

Existential Duality

This is how I do what I do. This is how I do my work as an off-world liaison. I put together into the title of off-world liaison several activities which could also be called multi-dimensional states. What this means is that sometimes I am a human on earth, and sometimes I am not. The term I use for sometimes being a human on earth and sometimes not is Existential Duality.

Most people cannot do this consciously. I don't know if anyone else can do this, until I do what my off-world contacts are telling me we can do together, it hasn't been done, not lately anyway.

Most people cannot be conscious without their body. Some people remember their dreams. Some people even realize they are dreaming sometimes. Beyond that, not much. I've been wondering for most of my life why no one is aware of these experiences.

But for the 9 multi-dimensional states I describe here, I don't know of anyone else who participates like this. I'm sure I can't be the only one. Most humans who can do this just don't come back to being a human again, they're done and on to new horizons.

And don't get me wrong, this is not easy. Try it for yourself. These are the most difficult tasks I know of. Most people who try just give up, it's not possible for them, anyway.

When I am visit heaven while I'm still alive, I get asked every time, "How can you be here? How can you do this?"

When I put in a request to an alien species, they will come, I have some favors I can call in, but I don't like to do it, I don't want to do it, this is not easy stuff, at least not with my skills.

When I work with energetic bodies, I see the cause of conditions. I sometimes get sick, due to the sickness of the energetic body I did work on. They make it look exciting in the movies, but you must know what you are doing, and a lot of the time you're just clueless.

In this healing work, I was working on a woman with chronic pain, specifically in her shoulder. My contacts told me to pass on to her not to call it her shoulder, call it her should-er, she keeps saying in her mind, "I should have…"

So, I got her pain to go away, and that was the first time in a long time, so she was just thrilled for a little relief. Was it in her head? To paraphrase Dumbledore, "Of course it's in your head, just because it's in your head doesn't mean it isn't real."

Someone who doesn't believe in what I do knew the woman didn't lie, and even though he didn't have a box to put it in, asked me how I did it. I couldn't really answer because I don't really do it, I'm just the tool used by whoever is doing it, I'm just a conduit for energy and truth in that work.

When I work with entities, I always feel like a fool. My concerns and efforts, even to help save the planet, are puny. I've even had entities tell me that those I was asking for help are not really interested. Great.

When I get acquisitions, when I'm given symbols, it's still like being hit with a 2x4 to the head.

When I say I can get you the technology I'm talking about, you need to know I need the energy of many people. And this is not electricity, that's a drop in the bucket compared to the energy I need. The energy I need is maybe a million times stronger than the electricity a city uses. And the tough part is, you don't even know the energy exists. You can't detect it with your eyes and senses.

I'm in the fun position of telling you to help me with your energy. The case to get help is made automatically when activated because those sparks make a big impression. In other words, I need you to activate yourself, and the result is real. But I must help you activate you in the proper way. To that end, they gave me the 3 conditions. This is the simplest way they could figure out to cleanly activate a human.

They say with 3 million properly activated we can do almost anything. We have nearly 300 million in America, so that's 1 in 100. Let's get to it.

So, how do I get there from here. I present the progression in this transmission. Here are the 10 multi-dimensional states as I know them:

1. Death

2. Near Death Experience

3. Lucid Dreaming

4. Out of Body Experience

5. Visiting Heaven

6. Aliens Encounters

7.   Energetic Body

8.   Entities

9.   Acquisition

10.   Bilocation

There are multi-dimensional states with good documentation available, and to these I have added states which have different focuses. The first 4 have quite a bit of documentation, there are books you can read. For the last 6, they represent different focuses. I didn't know I was doing them until they happened, again and again. To accomplish the last 6, it is true you must be able to focus appropriately. This ability is developed over centuries, so if you can do these, you started a long time ago.

People may have not had any of these experiences, so this is just a strange illusion from a mental case...me. As one has these experiences and studies them, the differences between the types of experiences are learned.

I've been studying these experiences for many lifetimes, and I go back and forth between different lifetimes. While time marches on, this is not how I experience it anymore. And when I come back to this life, sometimes I don't know where I am, I may not even know my gender and that can be concerning. It all comes back quickly, and on occasion I've commented, "Who am I?" or "Damn, I'm back here again." Or the scariest, "When in time am I now?"

In the physical world, time marches on, moment by moment. The prior lives are long gone here. When I look for the towns or villages in which I have lived, they are gone. This is when it can dawn on you, the physical world is just a temporary one. It's just like Lao-Tzu said so long ago: it's an illusion.

I still have my prior lives, I still have all those experiences, they are only gone in the mill in which they were churned out, the physical universe.

I still like parts of my last life more than this one, even though I have better skills this time. I can still remember my house I had in Canada, around Banff. I can draw the layout. It had a central grand room of dark wood that is still my favorite room. I remember the color of the drapes and where the hole in the roof was. I ended up there after I went to the Yukon for the gold rush. I didn't get much gold, just enough to buy a house and live on. Jack London was there, too, and he wrote a book about these skills. But you don't have to go to prison to do it, that just made sense to him because you must shut out this world for a continuous period of time.

The physical universe creates these realities to the beat of a drum: time. But when you look at time not as a series of seconds, but as a series of centuries, your perception of time and the physical universe changes. I see the universe churning out these sets of experiences, but when one is done, the next starts. When that is done, the next starts. Pretty soon, I have all these sets of experiences we would call lifetimes. But when you step back, they stop being linear, and are more like rows.

As you comprehend the symbols within the lives, you see that the symbols have connection to other symbols. For example, this is not that difficult to understand, in one life I was a son, in another life I had a son, in another life I lost a son, in another life I adopted a son. Son is the symbol. Son exists as a group of thoughts and emotions.

The physical aspect was experienced and ended. The sensory record still exists if you want to experience any part of it again. But the energy is thought and emotion, and it is observable and quantifiable if you have the ability. Every thought and emotion which is part of son. These thoughts and emotions are everything which I felt and thought.

So, not a sentimental parade. Anger, frustration, and pain are as common as love. But in the energetic realm, you see the stronger energy, exponentially stronger, is the love. And just like in the physical universe, the definition of love is not singular. The definition I have appreciated, and use is where love can be seen as 4 actions: giving, receiving, respecting, and appreciating.

The connections are automatic, but you must discern them. This is your purpose between lives. For most of us in most of our lifetimes, this is how we learn, after the life is over, we go over it all and figure out what the hell happened.

But you cannot experience time as a series of centuries while being subject to the beat of time's drum, second by second. With time beating like a drum, you still have your own drumbeat: your beating heart. With every beat of your heart, your body flashes a group of sensory inputs accompanied by a thought or feeling , your stream of consciousness while you simultaneously perceive the world. In this way, you create a movie, a series of flashes equal to your heartbeat.

This is the creation of your experience. With the next beat of your heart, the last flash is replaced by the new flash. While alive we never get to go back; this movie does not have a remote control with pause and rewind. The moments may be saved in our memory, or not.

When you step out of time, that movie stops. When you can look around for a bit without the movie of experiencing your life, you can understand: the drum of time does not beat itself, there is the one who beats the drum, there is the designer who creates time. And the designer of time is not subject to time, they created it for their purposes, but we are subject to time.

One of those purposes is to enable a continuous experience for a soul, you, as a human being. The purpose of this experience as a human being is to experience what it is you experience: your feelings, your thoughts, your beliefs, and your experiences. That's it, that's the purpose of life. You didn't miss it; you are living it. People may want to argue or discuss about the purpose of life, and this is fine, this is one of their purposes.

But one day, and it will happen to all of us, this experience will end. And when you walk through that door, you go through the door alone. Now that sounds scary, and it is. But on the other side of the door of death, everyone you knew who went before is waiting for you, so it's all good.

For most people, this is when the learning starts. When we live a life, we are so focused upon the world we experience and what we must do, and what we want to do, that we do not learn much. We don't know what the experience means, we don't know why we had the experience, we don't know why this or that happened. We had to make a choice and we did, not knowing if it was the right choice or not.

And then the drum beat of time pushes us to the next situation with which we must deal. When this life ends for us, this is when we start learning. It would be nice if we could learn while we are living the life, but usually we are just too busy trying to survive, make our plans happen, and getting through the day. So, we don't.

When you have a physical body and senses, these senses define your world. When you do not have a body and are conscious, you can access a larger universe. It's not a given, but it can be done. The important knowledge is that this is not an unnatural experience. Even more importantly, it's not a illusion. It may seem to be an illusion here,

271

but it's not an illusion where I live, it's my experience.

The perception of this physical universe was designed and created. This perception must be learned, and the initial period of our lives is where we learn this perception, normally our first two years. We learn how to focus upon this reality, and then it is not something which is simply happening to us while we look around, it becomes a place where we can do stuff.

When your heart stops and you stop breathing, that perception ends. It is a forced ending and is experienced as being abrupt. This is the death experience.

There are those whose bodies die, for example, after a heart attack. They are technically dead for a minute or two, and then their heart is restarted. Often, while dead, these people have the same experience as death, which is that they are partially disconnected from their body. When your heart stops and you stop breathing, you will have this experience. When the heart restarts, they breathe again, they re-attach to their body and regain consciousness.

This is called a near-death experience, or NDE. If you don't regain consciousness, it's a death experience. You must die and come back to life to have a near-death experience. There is no guarantee that you will come back, your body may be revived. So, this is not a good method for daily use.

The third type of multi-dimensional experience is lucid dreaming. With Lucid Dreaming, you are conscious while dreaming. You know it's a dream.

The fourth type of multi-dimensional experience is called an out-of-body-experience, or OOBE. In an out-of-body experience, you are aware that you are out of your body and can navigate this or another world, not just a dream landscape.

So, in this experience, you are not in a dream landscape, you are in the world. However, your abilities are limited- you can perceive the world, but you don't have a physical body to take significant actions. Through will, there have been minor physical actions, such as moving objects a little bit. This is the same as paranormal videos.

The fifth stage of multi-dimensional experience is what I call visiting heaven. The difference between visiting heaven and residing there is that the residents have adjusted and are comfortable, and I'm just trying to get my bearings. This is the first stage where my experiences seem to differ from others.

Many who have had a near-death experience also visit heaven, during the NDE but also afterwards. People who have not had a NDE can and do visit heaven. But they may not remember it, or they may not understand what they experienced. The NDE becomes the opening of a door to the multi-dimensional experience.

In visiting heaven, I visit people I know whose bodies have died. Many are very surprised, because I don't think they have seen a living person conscious in heaven. They usually ask me how I do it and say something like I'm not supposed to be able to do that.

I'm really not that good at it, I mean, I can see how I could be better at it. I get confused, I lose my way, I get distracted, I make small talk instead of getting what I'm there for, stuff like that.

The next stage of this type of experience is working with what you would call aliens. They come when I summon them, but I don't really like these guys. They aren't typically built like humans, so they don't understand the nature of our bodies.

So, for example, some don't have pain, so you can operate on them while they watch, for instance.

It's not a big deal till they want to see how you are built. "We'll put you back together the way you are after we're done" is not much comfort.

I call this a different type of experience, and a unique one, because for me it is. When you make contact with these guys, they are the only ones in the room. You better know what you want, and if at all possible, be quick about it.

The next stage of this type of experience is working with my energetic body. My great teacher Yogananda was also able to do this type of work. I don't know that I'm closer to anyone than Yogananda, maybe my mom. At this level, you work with your energetic body and can observe it. This is how Yogananda was able to end his life on demand to show the west this truth.

It is common to call the connection of the soul to the body a silver cord. But it's not silver, it's energy. If you sever this cord you will die, but you must know how to do this as Yogananda did. That's more skill than I have. And the silver cord is only a small part of your energetic body, the connection between you and the energetic body which is controlling the body.

The next stage of this type of experience is to interact with entities. In Christian texts, these beings were called archangels. I have visited where they reside, but it was only because we wanted to see if I could handle it. I couldn't. I'm not worthy.

If I could have handled it, I think I would be a much better off-world liaison, but I might not have come back here, too. There are a few waiting for me in heaven to give it another go, but I want to help humans first. At least, I must publish the transmissions. If anyone wants to get any of the stuff I can access, great.

The next experience is acquisition, for example, to work with others for the purpose of acquisition of tech. This is our goal. For this, we need a real big village, and my challenge is to enable you to activate yourself properly. How big a group is what we are studying.

Technically, a hundred thousand humans would do if they were properly activated. But I question if everyone in a group will be properly activated. At what level of diminished activation does the activation no longer work? At what level does the size of the group enable activation of everyone. So these are Activation parameters which are a bit different for every free will species.

For safety, we are thinking that 1 million for a goal might work, and we're pretty sure that 3 million will work. That's our project.

The final experience is bilocation. This is like OOBE, except you manifest an image of yourself where you are located, which is not where your body is located, and can interact with those who are there. The most advanced ability is to interact with people who are there. You have the similar physical abilities as OOBE, meaning you cannot do much.

I have not mastered this state. My training and skill set is focused on off-world abilities, so I haven't focused on OOBE and bilocation as much as acquisition.

These are the analyses the scientists I work with are studying off-world. It's a big project, a species can only go extinct once, and so the best shot is like, right now, when humans are closing in on the point of no return and enough humans can feel it, they know it.

There are the resources to do this. We added up everything and all the projects cost less than $200 billion, and the yield will be at least $2 trillion a year, so 10:1 annual return, or 1000%. So, we can do this. And this is just the return for investors. We estimate 10x increase in income for the most people. So, if you earn less than average household income, multiply your income by 10 to get our estimate of your potential income.

To do this, we use universal connections and symbols. This is my part of the project. These are the tools of the trade.

Normally, the off-world source with whom we work has significant experience. The information is passed exchanged in symbols.

For a breathing human, the concept of symbols is the best I can do to describe the mechanism of communication off-world. This is important because symbols are how we can acquire technology and solutions. Symbols are the containers. The symbols, as well, have associated threads. These threads lead to other symbols.

Symbols of these types exist in the context of the individuals who created the symbol and their basis for the symbol. The symbol is what is passed in the contact with the individual who has created the symbol.

For solutions, which are different from technology, the off-world sources can work with threads, which are multi-connections, like a neuron which connects to multiple neurons.

To Stop Extinction

As you can imagine, threadwork is quite complex, and quickly expands beyond workability, so we zoom in and out, in and out, and try not to lose the thread in the confusion of a dozen of options.

Think of Antman in the quantum realm, and I'm supposed to navigate this kaleidoscope, make a connection off-world, and have them hand me over some tech.

That's where you come in, with you guys on the project and being clear about what you want, they don't even ask, it's amazing, they already know what I'm there for, they just hand it over, and I'm out of there. With any luck, I can make it work once I'm back. That's the plan.

Tech seems easy compared to solutions. But I don't have to bring back something technical, so that is simpler. With a solution, I must go off-world, find the ones who can help the solution take place.

Then I have to come back to earth, find them, convince them, and we get a solution. But it's not just one person, it's a bunch of people who don't work with each other and are all over the place. Think of that Tom Cruise movie, Edge of Tomorrow, no matter how hard he tried, he couldn't convince the general to do something the general didn't want to do. That's how it is. But, again, your energy changes that like magic, if I a million help we've got a solution.

Summary

These types of experiences exist where a human is conscious and active without a body:

1. Death

2. Near Death Experience

3. Lucid Dreaming

4. Out of Body Experience

5. Visiting Heaven

6. Aliens Encounters

7. Energetic Body

8. Entities

9. Acquisition

10. Bilocation

The last six of this list will be used in this project, depending on the requirements of the project. There are two parts: acquisition off-world using one of these methods, and activation of humans.

Transmission

A transmission is the translation of a symbol into language. For example, when you feel love for someone, you translate this feeling into language, and may say or think, "I love you."

A symbol is an off-world concept. A symbol contains all supporting documentation. The translation of a symbol can go into as much detail or as little detail as desired. Some are small, with only a little translation required. Others are enormous.

I have had to decide how much of each symbol to translate so that a complete understanding can be achieved. If a translation is not adequate, please let me know and I can take another look at the symbol. I can add more to the transmission for the next version.

While this makes it seem like the symbol is a physical object, it is not. Additionally, the symbol typically has links to other souls and other symbols.

To Stop Extinction

To me, this is like depictions of neurons in the human brain with their several connections to other neurons.

Symbols

So, off-world we don't have memos. Memos are something you can say you didn't get. Off-world, information is there, all you do is think about a subject and you get all the information, more info than you can handle in the next decade if you study full time.

I call this information a symbol. I had to pick a name or a description, so symbol works. Symbol in this context means all the information about a subject.

A symbol might include background info, history, probable pasts, comparative situations, every possible plan, all opinions, all analyses, all options, probabilities, probable realities, likely participants, participants behavior, participants contribution, with an alternative participants list that could be a thousand names on it with probable realities for each of their behaviors and contributions. Then there are connections to entire cultures of people who are oblivious to the situation and program because they choose to be. However, an asteroid hitting the planet will affect the dinosaur even if he does not care and pays no attention.

Made in United States
Troutdale, OR
12/17/2023

15988317R10169